LIFE IN ANCIENT ROME

LIFE IN ANCIENT ROME

JOAN P. ALCOCK

First published 2010

The History Press
The Mill, Brimscombe Port
Stroud, Gloucestershire, GL5 2QG
www.thehistorypress.co.uk

© Joan P. Alcock, 2010

British Library Cataloguing in Publication Data.
A catalogue record for this book is available from the British Library.

ISBN 978 0 7524 4800 8

Typesetting and origination by The History Press
Printed in Great Britain

For Margaret and Jonathan Hardwick,
good friends who always provide
hospitality when needed.

CONTENTS

ACKNOWLEDGEMENTS

I am grateful to Stephen Kern, Barbara Kern and Maureen Walshe for their help in correcting the manuscript and assisting with this book. Linda Ward has provided the drawings of artefacts and the maps. All images are copyright of the author unless otherwise specified. The author is grateful to the friends who have contributed some photographs and given her their copyright.

INTRODUCTION

Ancient Rome, both as a republic and as an empire, continues to enthral and fascinate us. From a small settlement, Rome expanded to become a great empire stretching from the Atlantic to Asia Minor and from North Africa to the northern parts of Europe. When St Luke wrote that 'Caesar Augustus sent out a decree that all the world should be taxed' he meant the whole Roman world as it was in his time. Yet this did not encompass later territory gains, including provinces under Roman control and areas outside the empire, which became client states.

Evidence of Roman trade has been found from Ireland to China and goods poured into Rome making it a vast trading emporium. Rome influenced later civilisations so that the Latin language became the basis of other languages and many words employed today for officials and institutions are derived directly from Latin and their use in Rome. There is an empathy between Rome and our own times, which seems to strike a chord with many people. The portraits and sculptures in museums seem familiar to us; the artefacts, locked now in cases, could be in use today – sandals, boots, surgical instruments, tools and jewellery.

Much of the evidence for the Roman world comes from architectural remains, graffiti, reliefs, tombstones and other objects. Inscriptions give a glimpse of the thoughts, the lives and careers of these people. Even more important, Latin literature and the words of historians, politicians, geographers, gossips and raconteurs provide a portrait of a society, which is at the same time alien and familiar – cruel and kind, honourable and corrupt, bureaucratic and benevolent, witty and sarcastic.

Pliny the Younger's letters to his friends and officials reveal his kindness, prejudice, deference to authority and his interest in his world. Pliny the Elder left a geographical description of the natural world. Cato, Columella and Varro give clear instructions on farming practices and the management of estates. Frontinus, Vitruvius and Vitellius provide the official view with their manuals on strategy and technicalities. Galen, Celsius and Hippocrates contribute medical manuals, which showcase their medical knowledge and how this could relieve illness and cope with accidents. Dio Cassius, Strabo, Tacitus and Dionysius of Halicarnassus provide the historical background. Caesar's account of his conquests indicates his determination for recognition and his overwhelming ambition. Cicero's writings proclaim his passion for justice.

Ovid gives us descriptions of religious practices, rites and evidence of love affairs. Horace tells us about his daily life. Suetonius provides a history of the lives of the emperors. Petronius, Juvenal and Martial are great gossips and satirists.

The Romans, secure in their own world, were able to enjoy life, record it and to mock it, but only up to a point. Several writers were exiled for their satires and others committed suicide, either through fear or on command due to imperial displeasure; life could be fragile.

This book concentrates on life lived in Italy mainly in the late republic and the empire. Examples are taken from the city of Rome, the excavated towns of Pompeii and Herculaneum and the abandoned town of Ostia, but with reference to life in other parts of the empire. It is impossible to understand Rome without some knowledge of its government and administration. Throughout the empire, towns and cities elected councils and officials based on those in Rome. Roman law, with some additions of local custom, governed all provinces in the empire. There was toleration, with some exceptions, of religious cults and practices in other parts of the empire. Those who wished to be considered Roman citizens enthusiastically embraced Roman customs, education, entertainments and other habits, and Romanisation was encouraged as part of a civilising process. In AD 212 citizenship was extended to all parts of the empire to ensure loyalty to one central government.

The Romans, with perhaps overweening arrogance, assumed that it was their destiny to conquer other peoples and created a great empire. Yet, there was a sense of security and of being protected within that empire. When it began to crumble in the fifth century AD it must have seemed like the ending of the world.

1

THE CITY: KINGDOM, REPUBLIC, EMPIRE

'Not without reason', said Livy 'have gods and men chosen this site for the founding of the city.' Rome was situated on the River Tiber, 30km (18.5 miles) from its mouth, where the river was crossed by a ford just below an island in the middle of the river. Tiber Island survives today as a ridge of alluvium. The ford was a crucial factor in the development of the prosperity of the city as the crossing attracted people to the area, while the island provided a useful place to offload goods for both shipment and surface transportation. Unfortunately the land was also liable to flood and the problem was not solved until embankments were built in the nineteenth century.

Here the Romans built the first bridge, the Pons Sublicius, across the Tiber, which according to Livy was constructed by King Ancus Marcius and was protected by fortifications of the Janiculum. A *sublica* is a wooden pile and this was a wooden bridge that because of a religious ban on the use of metal was constructed entirely without nails. A later bridge, the Pons Aemilius, lasted until it was destroyed by floods in the sixteenth century and one archway of it survives just below Tiber Island. That bridge was probably built in the mid-third century BC to connect with the making of the Via Aurelia, which led into Etruria.

Because the lowland area was subject to flooding, early settlements were placed on the surrounding hills.

The Pons Aemilius (Ponte Rotto) was the first stone bridge to be built over the Tiber. This bridge was a rebuilding by Augustus after a previous bridge had been destroyed. Several times damaged and repaired, some of the bridge was destroyed by floods in 1598. Two of the other three arches were destroyed in the 1880s leaving this single arch

One on the Capitoline Hill is known to have existed from the fourteenth century BC; another was on the Palatine. The population grew because it attracted traders and was a connecting link between the Greek colonies in the south and the Etruscans in the north. The city therefore flourished especially after Ancus Marcius founded the port of Rome at Ostia and destroyed all the settlements between that area and Rome in order to ensure the city's prosperity.

ROMULUS AND REMUS

The founding of Rome is inextricably tied up with the legend of Romulus and Remus, which both Livy and Virgil recounted in their writings. The Romans traced their origins to Aeneas who escaped the destruction of Troy, landed on the coast of Latium and married the daughter of a Latin king. Aeneas founded a city and his son Ascanius created the kingdom of Alba Longa in the Alban Hills. A later king Proclus, on his death, divided the kingdom between his sons. Amulius drove out his brother Numitor, and prevented his brother's daughter Rhea Silvia from marrying by making her a priestess. She, however, having been raped by the god Mars, gave birth to twin sons, Romulus and Remus.

She was imprisoned; the boys were put into a boat and set adrift on the river but their boat grounded near a fig tree. Here they were found by a wolf that suckled them before a shepherd Faustulus saw them and took them back to his wife Laurentia to rear. Once they had reached manhood they ranged widely for game, and as they shared their booty with others they gathered together a large following. Emboldened by this the brothers moved against Amulius, killed him, restored Numitor to the throne and decided to build a city in the area where they had been brought up. Soon emigrants from the Alban and Latin states joined them and, as Livy said, 'they all hoped that Alba would be small and Lavinium small as compared with the city

A bronze of a she-wolf and twins. The wolf was cast in Etruria in the fifth century BC. Antonio del Pollaiolo added the twins around 1509 to enhance the legend of the foundation of Rome. (Musei Capitolini, Rome)

The head of the she-wolf

they should build.' But these considerations were 'interrupted by the curse of their forefathers – the greed for kingly power' – and an ugly struggle broke out between the brothers.

As the twins did not know who was the oldest they decided to choose by augury who should give the city a new name and govern it. Romulus took his place on the Palatine, Remus on the Aventine. Remus saw a flight of six vultures but then 12 appeared to Romulus. Each claimed the victory but 'they then engaged in a battle of words and angry taunts leading to bloodshed'. Remus was struck down in the affray. Livy said that Remus leapt over the wall to mock his brother whereupon Romulus in great anger slew him, and in menacing wise added these words, 'so perish all whosoever else shall leap over my wall' Thus Romulus acquired power, and the city was called after its founder's name.

Dionysius of Halicarnassus and Ovid both said that Remus had reluctantly yielded the leadership to Romulus before leaping over the wall saying, 'Well, as for this wall, one of your enemies could as easily cross it as I do', whereupon he was killed by Celer, the overseer of the wall.

The detail of the stories and the naming of all the participants do suggest that this legend, passed down orally, had some degree of truth. The traditional date for the founding of Rome 753 BC is also very precise. Whatever happened, Romulus decided to fortify the Palatine Hill, 'on which,' said Livy, 'he had been reared', and ploughed a furrow to indicate the area of the city. The hut of Romulus and the Lupercal Cave, the legendary site where the twins had been reared, located between the Circus Maximus and the flood plain, became revered places for the Romans. Augustus, as part of his policy of linking himself with the original founder of Rome and as founder of a new Rome, stated that he rebuilt the cave, which implies that it was by then some form of grotto.

Archaeologists have discovered traces of Iron Age huts in the area and a small enclosure may have preserved some form of structure that the Romans honoured as being the home of the city's founder. Dionysius of Halicarnassus said that Romulus and Remus built their huts entirely out of wooden poles and reeds; 'One of these, called the hut of Romulus, survives almost to my day, on the flank of the Palatine Hill which faces towards the Circus Maximus and it is preserved by those who have charge of it.' He stated that if damaged it was replaced and restored to its former structure. He added that it was burnt down in 12 BC when crows dropped burning sacrificial meat on it which they had stolen from a nearby altar. Seneca, however, refers to the 'humble hut of Romulus' being honoured on the Capitoline below the Temple of Jupiter.

Romulus was reported to have died about 716 BC or to have disappeared or been taken away by Mars, his reputed father, in a mist which came during a thunderstorm, while he was holding a muster on the Campus Martius. Livy, Dionysius and Ovid are more sceptical saying that his own people killed him. Livy pointed the finger at the senators who were engaged in a struggle for the coveted leadership, while Dionysius asserted that they were incensed because Romulus had released some hostages whom he had taken from the Veientes and that he treated people who had joined the city population earlier with more honour than those who had joined later. He was also cruel, punishing delinquents by throwing them down from a precipice (the Tarpeian Rock) so that he seemed to be exercising his power more like a tyrant than a king. Dionysius gave details of the senators attacking him in the Senate House, dividing his body into small pieces, each one holding a piece hidden in his robe and afterwards burying them in secret. The Black Stone (*Lapis Niger*) in the Forum near the Arch of Septimius Severus has older stones lying beneath it and this was claimed by Festus, a fourth-century AD writer, as the 'burial place of Romulus before he disappeared and made his burial impossible'. He also gave an alternative explanation that it was the burial place of the shepherd, Faustulus, who had been killed while trying to stop the brothers fighting.

A model of a turf and timber hut believed to represent the hut of Romulus

Romulus's supposedly prophetic last words were related by Proculus Julius who decreed that power had descended to him saying 'Declare to the Romans the will of heaven that my Rome shall be the capital of the world; so let them cherish the art of war, and let them know and teach their children that no human strength can resist Roman arms.' This the Romans certainly proceeded to do. But no excuse was needed. Roman writers took up the theme later indicating that Rome's destiny was to be ruler of the world. Virgil made Jupiter declare, 'I set upon the Romans neither bounds of space nor of time'. Rome should rule all peoples, impose the ways of peace, spare the defeated but crush proud men who would not submit. Livy had stated bluntly: 'The city of Rome shall be the capital of the entire world ... neither men nor power shall be able to resist the military might of Rome.'

EXPANSION OF THE CITY

The city grew in strength and expanded. Settlements occupied the Palatine and the Esquiline Hills as early as the ninth century BC. The other hills were also gradually settled because they offered safety from floods. Strictly speaking the hills of Rome were not hills as such but ridges created by streams running down the edges of valleys towards the river. The Seven Hills of Rome (*Septem Montes*) were commemorated in an annual festival called the *Septimontium* held on 11 December each year, which began about the first century BC. According to Scullard these seven hills were the Palatine, Velia, Fagutal, Cermalus, Caelian, Oppian and Cispian, not the more famous later seven hills. This indicates an expansion from the Palatine and the Esquiline but not far enough to include the Aventine, Quirinal and Viminal and curiously not the Capitol. Festus said that sacrifices were offered in 106 BC on each of the Seven Hills, the most important being on the Palatine where the Diva Palatua had a shrine with her own *flamen Palatualis*. Later Suetonius said that the Emperor Domitian celebrated the *Septimontium* with a banquet (*epulum*). The festival was still being performed in the third century AD as Tertullian mentioned it. By the first century AD, however, the Seven Hills were presumed to be the Aventine, Caelian, Capitoline, Esquiline, Palatine, Quirinal, and the Viminal, while in the fourth century AD the Vatican and the Janiculum had replaced the Quirinal and the Viminal.

Central Italy had three distinct groups – the Latins on the right side of the Tiber, the Etruscans to the north and the Sabines to the west. These regularly formed alliances with each other and kept contact with the Greeks, who had colonised southern Italy, and with traders from other parts of the Mediterranean. Rome tended to dominate the area, regularly conquering land and people as witnessed by legends such as the rape of the Sabine women, which masks the wars against that people. When Rome was under attack by her neighbours, the military system she established enabled her to guard and expand her territory.

Rome defeated the Latins at Lake Regillus in 494 BC and then the Volsci. The Etruscan city of Veii was captured in 396 BC after a 10-year siege, leading to more territory being taken. In the south, Campania and the Bay of Naples came under Roman control and the Greek stronghold of Taranto fell in 272 BC. The only check on this seemingly inevitable expansion was the Gauls who had swept from the north to attack Rome in the fourth century. They reached Rome, sacked the city and would have captured the Capitol had their night climb not disturbed the sacred geese dedicated to Juno whose cackling alerted the garrison.

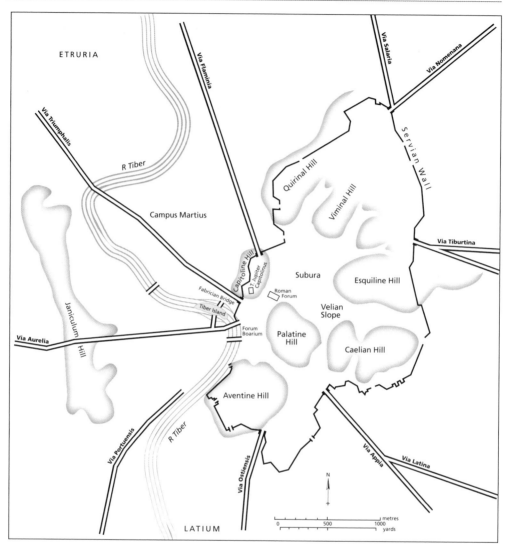

Map of the Seven Hills of Rome

The Gauls withdrew after extracting a ransom but this was regarded as a temporary setback to expansion.

At first Rome was ruled by legendary kings, who constructed many of the monuments and facilities of Rome – the Marmetine Prison, the great drainage system the Cloaca Maxima, the Circus Maximus and the Temple of Jupiter on the Capitol, which was attributed to Romulus but which was extended in the sixth century BC to become the huge temple of Jupiter Optimus Maximus with additional shrines to other deities.

As the power of Rome grew and she attracted more people to her for protection and trade, large aristocratic houses were built, some of which have been excavated under the granaries of Vespasian. Rome was divided into four administrative districts – Collina, Palatina, Esquilina and Suburana – which were enclosed by a wall in the sixth century BC, reconstructed as the

Servian Wall in the fourth century BC. The area enclosed was about 425 hectares which made it the largest city in Italy and Livy said that a census undertaken by Servius in the sixth century BC reported that some 80,000 citizens lived there, many being newcomers. Dionysius said that Servius enlarged the city with the addition of the Esquiline and the Quirinal.

EXPANSION OF CIVIC AMENITIES

The Cloaca Maxima enabled swampy land to be drained so that a large civil area, the Forum, could be laid down between the Capitoline and the Esquiline. Ovid recalled meeting an old woman who told him about the marshy area of the Forum: 'Here where the Forums now are was once wet swamps, a ditch drenched with water washed back from the river.' The Forum Romanum was the focal point for all political and religious activity. It was a stage for political trials and urban spectacles such as public feasts. Throughout the republic and the empire, buildings continued to be altered, destroyed and replaced, except in a few cases such as that of

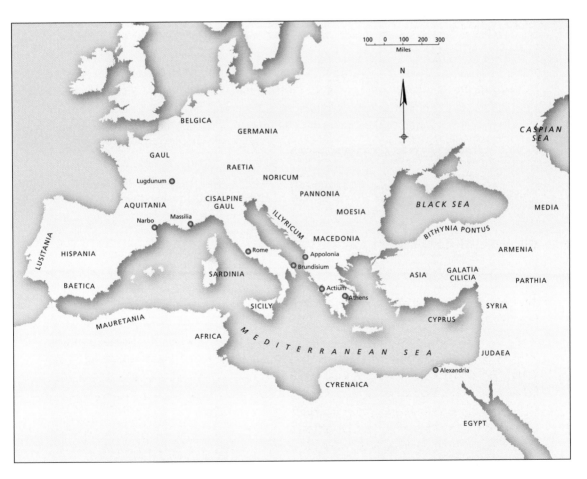

Map of Italy in the third and fourth centuries BC

the Senate House, so that in late empire the Forum had a very different appearance compared to what it looked like during the republic.

The last king was expelled in 509 BC, the date at which a republic was declared, and building continued. This included the temples of Salus and Castor and Pollux in the Forum and the temples to Ceres and Mercury by the Aventine. The Temple of Apollo was founded on the Campus Martius and the Villa Publica housed a newly created officer, the censor. Civic amenities were added. The huge aqueducts, the Appia and the Anio Vetus were provided in 312 BC and 272 BC respectively. The Appia entered Rome at the Porta Maggiore, went along the Aventine and brought water to Forum Boarium close to the Tiber. Calculations suggest that it could deliver 73,000m³ of water a day. The Anio also entered Rome at the Porta Maggiore but then went along the Esquiline to the Viminal delivering 173,000 m³ of water a day.

After the invasion of the Gauls it was realised that the defences of the city needed strengthening. A complete reconstruction of the walls was ordered. This was begun in 378 BC and completed around the 350s. There was also a requirement to ensure that travel was made easier through Italy. Thus the first of an extremely competent road system was begun, the Via Appia, laid out on the order of the Censor, Appius Claudius Caecus. This reached Capua about 312 BC and was extended to Brundisium by 272 BC.

Rome was already expanding her territories further. She had tried to make her enemies into allies and to co-opt them into joining her military forces by offering them a share of the booty and giving them control over their own areas. But extension into Sicily in 264 BC brought her into contact with Carthage which controlled a trading empire in the Mediterranean. Rome had no compunction in attempting to eliminate Carthaginian power. The First Punic War lasted until 241 BC. By the end of it Rome had built up a formidable navy, which aimed to control the Mediterranean. Hannibal then moved into the Iberian Peninsular from which he invaded

Italy in 218 BC. He was not defeated until 201 BC. By 146 BC Carthage had been finally defeated, the city razed to the ground and salt ploughed into her fields so that she would never recover. Africa became a new province and southern Gaul succumbed to Rome in 121 BC. Within the next 20 years Greece, most of the Aegean and large parts of Asia Minor and North Africa had become subject to Rome. The policy had become more offensive than defensive.

For Rome this meant that an enormous amount of booty – gold, silver, furniture

The mouth of the Cloaca Maxima where it entered the Tiber beneath the present embankment. It drained the valleys between the Esquiline, the Viminal and the Quirinal

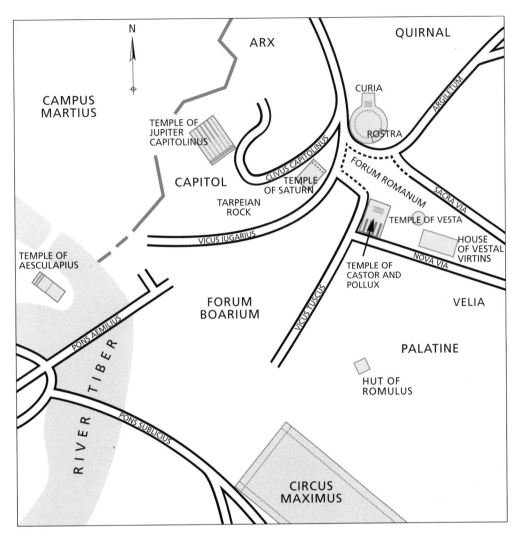

Plan of central Rome in the early Republic

and works of art – poured into the city. In addition skilled craftsmen, artists, philosophers, poets, even cooks arrived who would enhance the city and its lifestyle. Many of the artists and sculptors were from Greece and they passed on their knowledge to Roman craftsmen. So many statues were added to the city that it was said Rome had become a Greek city. This was also reflected in the building of temples, many of which followed the Greek model but with a raised podium.

There was also development in more practical areas. The Forum Holitorium (vegetable market) and the Forum Boarium (cattle market) provided useful space where trade could thrive. Ovid said that the latter took its name from the statue of an ox while Tacitus referred to a bronze bull dominating the site. New drainage systems were added and street paving first noted in the third century had become normal practice by the 170s. Two new aqueducts, the Marcian (140

Modern statue of Augustus placed alongside the Forum of Augustus

BC) and the Tepula (105 BC) brought an extra 200,000m³ of water a day to serve the growing population. Some was piped directly into buildings; most of it could be collected from the many fountains throughout the city. River wharves were extended and the Porticus Aemilius, a huge emporium where goods could be off-loaded, was rebuilt in concrete in 174 BC. New and better materials and especially marble from Italian, Greek and Near Eastern quarries were brought to enhance the appearance of public buildings.

The conflict of the Civil Wars in the first century BC delayed building projects. Even so Sulla ensured the paving of the Forum and Pompey built the first permanent theatre between 61 and 55 BC. A huge *porticus* was added attached to the annex in which the Senate sometimes held meetings. It was there that Julius Caesar was assassinated in 44 BC. Before his death Caesar had restored parts of the republican Forum, rebuilt the Senate House and the speaker's platform, begun to build a new basilica (the Julia) and laid out a completely new Forum which Augustus finished with a temple dedicated to Venus Genetrix. Cicero indicated that Caesar was planning a complete redesign of the city, even altering the course of the Tiber before his death, and the building of the new Forum enabled the emperors to put their mark on the city by adding their own forums.

EXPANSION IN THE EARLY EMPIRE

Once Octavian, Caesar's adopted heir, had defeated Mark Anthony at the Battle of Actium in 31 BC, he set about renewing republican virtues, but Dio Cassius shrewdly remarked that all power passed from the people and the Senate to him and that, from this time speaking, Rome was an empire. In 27 BC the Senate conferred on him the title of Augustus, which became the usual form of address for all future emperors. Augustus began a programme of reconstruction and restoration and also added grandiose concepts – the Forum of Augustus with the Temple of Mars Ultor (the Avenger), the Ara Pacis, and his own mausoleum. He divided the city into 14 regions under control of magistrates and wards under supervisors elected by the people. He organised corps of *vigiles* as firemen. He built his own house on the Palatine and added a Temple of Apollo, his preferred deity. On the Campus Martius he built temples, porticoes and other amenities. The four aqueducts were restored and two new ones, the Julia and the Virgo, were built which provided an extra 148,000m³ of water each day.

He had no hesitation in listing all his achievements on inscriptions (known as the *Res Gestae*), which were placed throughout the empire. These achievements included building and restoring 82 temples in Rome, a theatre, aqueducts, roads, bridges and gifts given from war booty. Suetonius said that 'Augustus improved the city so greatly that he could rightly boast that he had found it of brick and left it as marble.' Increasingly architecture followed an approved style: the classical Greek style but with the Corinthian column being a distinguishing feature.

The next five emperors continued Augustus's reconstruction. Two further aqueducts were added – the Claudia and the new Anio. Claudius's major work was the construction of a new seaport at the mouth of the Tiber. New forums were built, the imperial palace on the Palatine was enlarged and Nero built a large public market on the Caelian Hill.

Augustus had been concerned with public buildings. Squalid and slum buildings remained, but in June AD 64 a fire beginning in some shops besides the Campus Martius got out of control,

The Ara Pacis Augustae was erected in the Campus Martius by decree of the Senate after Augustus' victorious return from Spain and Gaul in July 13 BC and was finished in AD 9. It was reconstructed in 1938 from original fragments and re-erected near the original site

swept through the narrow streets and the timber houses and burned down a large part of the city. According to Tacitus little could be done to stop it, nor was Nero able to issue orders as he was in Antium and did not return until much of the Palatine had been consumed. On his return he built temporary structures for homeless people and brought in food supplies from neighbouring towns. Tacitus said, however, that 'all these efforts won Nero no favours since the rumour surfaced that while the city was still on fire he mounted his private stage to sing "The fall of Troy" comparing present calamities with ancient catastrophes.' Nero was even accused of starting the fire to further his own grandiose scheme.

In spite of the attempts of the *vigiles* the fire lasted nine days, destroying three regions and damaging another seven. Nero took the opportunity to rebuild, ordering streets to be widened, the height of houses to be restricted and more squares to be built. Stone was used in preference to wood and porticoes placed along new apartment blocks to allow firemen to access the upper stories. He created the Domus Aurea in a new imperial estate with a man-made lake with farms, gardens and vineyards. Suetonius said that there were lampoons made about the house and much resentment at its coverage of a large area.

Ironically the Domus Aurea was to provide an excellent building site for Vespasian's construction of the Coliseum in AD 80. Titus added the Baths of Titus in the former gardens, and statues, which Nero had collected for his palace from Greece and Asia Minor, adorned a new Temple of Peace. To commemorate Titus's victory over the Jews and the taking of Jerusalem in AD 70, Domitian erected a large arch in the Forum Romanum with scenes of the sacred objects being carried in procession in the triumph, which followed Titus's victory. Domitian vigorously continued building after a fire destroyed the Capitol in AD 80. He added a stadium, an Odeon and a porticus in honour of his father and brother. He built a new imperial Forum which was inaugurated by Nerva in AD 97 and extended the palaces on the Palatine.

Part of the frieze of the Ara Pacis Augustae showing the procession of the Imperial family

The triumphal procession of Titus displayed on an inner part of the Arch of Titus

GRANDIOSE BUILDING

In the second century Rome was hugely expanded. The largest development was the Forum of Trajan with a library surrounding a column commemorating Trajan's Dacian triumphs, the last province to be added to the empire. Dio Cassius said that Apollodorus of Damascus, who built the Forum, the Odeon and the gymnasium, was later put to death by Hadrian for seemingly insulting the emperor's plan of the Temple of Venus and Rome. Trajan also added large public baths, and a market complex, closely connected with his Forum, consisting of a set of independent units operating on three separate street levels interconnected by staircases. In AD 109 he ordered a new aqueduct to be built, the Traiana, whose waters also drove water mills outside Rome.

Hadrian's rule was significant for both Rome and the empire. After his accession in AD 117 he made a long tour of the frontier regions and defined the boundaries of the empire, Hadrian's Wall being his legacy in Britain. In Rome he built the Temple of Venus and Rome, his huge mausoleum which rivalled that of Augustus, the enormous villa near Tivoli and rebuilt the Pantheon. Antoninus Pius was less ambitious. His contribution was two temples, one dedicated to Hadrian, the other to Antoninus and his wife Faustina. His long reign was relatively peaceful but his successor Marcus Aurelius had to face risings on the eastern and northern frontiers

Streets on three levels provided access to the Markets of Trajan. There were 150 shops and a great two-storeyed hall

of the empire. He erected two columns, one to commemorate Antoninus Pius and the other to celebrate his victories over the Marcomanni in AD 172–173 and the Sarmatians in AD 174–175. He also commemorated these victories by a triumphal arch, but this was later destroyed and the panels inserted into an arch built by Constantine. In every panel the emperor's head has been re-cut to show the features of the new ruler. The legacy of Commodus, the last of the Antonines, was mainly games and banquets but he finished the building of Marcus Aurelius's column and added a huge stone temple to Jupiter on the Palatine.

After Commodus, there was a struggle for the empire from which Septimius Severus emerged to begin the Severan dynasty. A devastating fire in AD 191 led to the restoration of the Temple of Peace and the Temple of Venus and the Horrea Piperataria (pepper halls). A huge temple to Hercules and Bacchus was constructed on the Quirinal Hill. Of more practical value were the barracks for the imperial cavalry and new stations for the *vigiles*. A wing was added to the imperial palace on the Palatine. The Senate awarded Septimius an arch in AD 203 to commemorate his Parthian victories, which included the capture of Ctesiphon, the Parthian capital. The arch was the first major construction in the Forum Romanum since the reign of Hadrian and it sealed Severus's claim to the empire. A marble planimetric representation of the city was completed in AD 213 and covered the wall of the restored Temple of Peace. Fragments of this survive and indicate the names of the walls, aqueducts and some important buildings.

Above: The Temple of the Divine Hadrian, built on the Campus Martius, was dedicated by Antoninus Pius in AD 145. Parts of the marble decoration of the podium and the inner pedestals have survived and some are placed in the courtyard of the Palazzo dei Conservatori, Rome. This piece symbolically represents the provinces of Vindelica on the left and of Dacia on the right

Left: Portrait head of Hadrian

Right: The Arch of Septimius Severus was erected in the Forum Romanum in AD 203 in honour of the Emperor and his sons, Caracalla and Geta. The reliefs represent the emperor's victories over the Parthians and the Arabs

His son, Caracalla, added to the public amenities by building the huge Baths of Caracalla, with water supplied by the Antoniniana aqueduct (AD 210–215) which was completed by Alexander Severus. The Baths of Nero on the Campus Martius were refurbished and were served with water supplied by a new aqueduct, the Alexandrina in AD 226. Previously Elagabalus had built a temple dedicated to himself whom he equated with Sol Invictus and had laid out a new palace with its own circus and amphitheatre in the southeast part of the city.

DECLINE IN THE IMPORTANCE OF ROME

On the death of Alexander Severus in AD 235 the empire descended into almost constant warfare with usurpers trying to gain control and invaders pushing at the frontiers. Eventually the empire was divided into two by Diocletian who finally gained control in AD 291. He became emperor in the east and installed Maximian as emperor in the west. Two years later they each appointed a junior Caesar to help them in this task and to be their designated successors.

Map of the empire in the time of Hadrian

Pedestal base on the Arch of Constantine dedicated AD 315. The sculpture on the bases represents Victories and captives

The unrest had led to Aurelian building the huge Aurelian Walls in AD 270–275 to protect the city from a threatened invasion by the Germanic tribes who were active in Gaul and northern Italy. The wall, 8m (26ft) high, 3.5m (12ft) thick and with a square tower placed every 29.6m (97ft) (100 Roman feet) enclosed a circuit of almost 19km (12 miles). Thirty years later Maxentius was to heighten the parapet and after AD 401 Honorius remodelled the walls, almost doubling the height.

Diocletian visited Rome only once in AD 303. Maximian restored parts of the Roman Forum, the Curia and the Forum of Caesar that had been badly damaged in a fire in AD 283 and added a huge set of baths on the Viminal Hill, which were dedicated to Diocletian several years later. These continued in use until the sixth century AD.

In AD 305, however, Diocletian abdicated forcing Maximian to do the same. Power passed to Constantius and Galerius, but Constantius died the next year and Maxentius, Maximian's son, seized control of Rome. He called his father out of retirement but subsequent quarrels led to Constantine, Constantius's son becoming sole emperor in AD 312. Maxentius had tried to invest his reign with a series of dynastic projects. He added a huge basilica with an elegant vestibule in the Forum, rebuilt part of Hadrian's Temple of Venus and Rome and had begun to build a mausoleum for himself and a circus on the Appian Way. Constantine ignored the last two, but completed building work on the others. To commemorate his victory over Maxentius he built an arch utilising panels and sculpture from monuments of Trajan, Hadrian and Marcus Aurelius. Although ostensibly dedicated to the Senate, Constantine had it erected in AD 315, the tenth anniversary of his accession to the empire.

Constantine and his co-emperor Licinius divided the empire between them with Constantine basing himself in Milan rather than Rome. In AD 324 Constantine seized complete control, and forced Licinius to commit suicide. Licinius had based himself at Byzantium on the Bosporus and in AD 330 Constantine moved his court there, proclaiming it to be the New Rome and with great ceremony decreed that it should be called Constantinople. From thence forward, although Rome kept its status, power had shifted. After AD 312 when Constantine declared his conversion to Christianity, he ordered the building of several Christian churches in Rome, including the basilica, baptistery and residence for the Bishop of Rome at the Lateran and funerary basilicas at Christian cemeteries outside Rome.

He and his successors never contemplated moving the capital back to Rome, although in AD 357 Constantius II visited the city and marvelled at its buildings. If buildings were to be restored and kept in good repair, this was the task of the Roman aristocracy. In AD 374 and 376 orders were given that magistrates were not to give any money from the public purse for new building. In the next century Rome was to suffer occupation and destruction by Alaric the Goth and later by the Vandals, but it also suffered from the greed of its own citizens who used the great buildings as quarries of limestone and marble to enhance their own dwellings. Rome would continue to play a part in history and eventually recover to become the centre for the Christian faith but it was no longer the centre of an empire, which had once dominated the known western world.

2

GOVERNMENT AND ADMINISTRATION

Roman society was based on the rule of law and a system of social class within which a man could follow a distinctive career. In theory the authority behind the law was the Roman people (*populus Romanus*) acting as and voting in assemblies. The Greek historian Polybius, who lived in Rome and whose work focused on military and political affairs, asked at the beginning of his history, 'Who was there so worthless an individual that he would not wish to know by what means and under what system of polity the Romans have succeeded in subjecting nearly the whole of the inhabited world to their sole government – a thing unique in government.' Rome also provided a distinct career path which enabled men to achieve higher status and involve them in legal and administrative duties. Part of this career structure, including military experience, would be useful for anyone who engaged in the expansion of the empire. During the empire it provided, although the Roman state would not have appreciated it, service beyond the boundaries of Italy bringing men into contact with other areas and tribes whose experiences would be alien to their own.

CITIZENSHIP

There was, however, a clear distinction between Roman and non-Roman citizens. Citizenship was confined to adult free males and those registered on the census. At first it was confined to those living in the city of Rome. Very reluctantly Rome admitted inhabitants from other areas of Italy but refused to extend it to provincials. This was understandable as citizens were freed from certain types of taxation. Citizenship gave the right to vote and to stand for election as magistrates but it also made a man liable for military service. Citizens could not be punished without a trial before a Roman magistrate. This was apparent when St Paul in Jerusalem was about to suffer a beating on the order of a centurion. 'Is it lawful', he asked, 'for you to scourge a man that is Roman and uncondemned?' The centurion quickly informed his superior who told Paul that he had bought his freedom with a large sum but Paul replied that he was freeborn.

At once he had to be released and be given protection. Later when again he was arrested on an accusation of disturbing the peace of the empire he appealed to Caesar and had to be sent to Rome. Here he was allowed to live with one of the soldiers, obviously under some form of house arrest.

During the late republic and early empire Roman citizenship was expanded, often as a result of service to the state. It could be granted en masse to a town or community. It could also be granted to Roman auxiliaries and their families or to a provincial who had joined a legion, if a man was discharged honourably from the army usually after 25 years of service. It was not until AD 212 that Caracalla gave citizenship as a right to most people in the empire, not because he wished to extend their legal rights but because citizens were subject to inheritance tax and he needed the money for increases in soldiers' pay after the murder of Geta.

The state monitored the wealth of its citizens by holding a census every four or five years to assess details of private wealth, occupations and the amount of property. It was such a census, probably the most famous in history, which was recorded by St Luke, when 'there went out a decree from Caesar Augustus that all the world should be taxed and this taxing was made when Cyrenius was governor of Syria.' This dates it to Publius Sulpicius Quirinius being governor of Judaea and Syria in AD 6. Two censors registered citizens in tribes and centuries that were divided into five classes according to how much wealth and property was held. During the late republic and the empire, the census was extended to the provinces, which became the responsibility of the provincial governor. From the census returns taxes could be levied. From 167 BC the *tributum* was both a land tax and a poll tax levied on all provincials whether citizens or not. During the empire Roman citizens in Rome and Italy were exempt from the tribute unless there was an emergency. Augustus decreed in 6 BC that they were liable for an inheritance tax which was used to fund legionary veterans' resettlement.

PATRICIANS AND PLEBEIANS

Roman citizenship also divided on social class lines: patricians and plebeians. Patricians were the most privileged. During the republic qualification was by birth; only sons of patricians could be patricians. The law of the Twelve Tables compiled in 451 BC banned intermarriage between the classes although, according to Cicero and Livy, this was repealed four years later. Patricians monopolised all the highest priesthoods and political offices but this began to be challenged in the fourth century in the dispute known as the struggle of the Orders. At last the plebeians organised themselves sufficiently to elect their own assembly which by 457 BC elected 10 tribunes as their leaders. In 367 BC they were allowed to elect one of their number as a consul and providing a man had enough wealth he might become a senator. These then became a new class (*nobilitas*), which could keep a check on the plebeians.

As many patrician families refused to marry out of their class their birth rate declined. During the empire, in an effort to keep up numbers the emperors would grant patrician status to favoured individuals or those who had served the state well. They could pass on this right to their descendants.

The plebeians made up the mass of citizens. Many were clients of patricians and depended on their patronage. Some served in the army as a tribunus militum. Wealthier plebeians achieved

almost political equality with the patricians although their status was still regarded as being in the lower social order. The 10 tribunes accepted resolutions to be passed onto the Senate and in the fourth century BC the assembly had gained sufficient power for these resolutions to become law if the Senate accepted them. The tribunes watched the proceedings of the Senate from its open doors and could object to laws they would not accept by blocking this exit. This became so irritating that eventually they were allowed to sit and speak in the Senate and even proposed subjects for discussion.

SENATORS AND THE SENATE

Cicero believed that the early kings of Rome had created the Senate and that by the time of their demise the Senate felt sufficiently confident to rule in its place. The kings and later the consuls had chosen members, but by the *Lex Ovinia* passed between 339 and 318 BC they were chosen by the censors. Ex-magistrates were almost automatically selected. Membership could be for life providing a man was of good character and a man could be expelled only for severe misconduct. By the middle of the first century BC the number in the Senate was fixed at 300 but this was later increased. Senators had to be freeborn citizens. The main criteria appeared to be wealth with a property over 400,000 sesterces. Sulla increased the number of senators by adding men of equestrian rank and Caesar admitted even more by rewarding his own followers

The Forum Romanum with the Curia and the Arch of Septimius Severus. Julius Caesar had begun to build the Senate House in 50 BC. After his assassination Augustus finished it by 29 BC. Domitian restored it in AD 94. The building was destroyed by fire in AD 283 and rebuilt by Diocletian. It has survived because it was converted into the Church of San Adriano in AD 630

so that by the end of the republic it was probably about 1000. Augustus thought that this was too high and reduced the number to 600. Senators were distinguished by wearing a toga with a broad stripe (*latus clavus*) and having special shoes. In the empire their sons gained these privileges by right of birth. Their main wealth was in land and they were not allowed to trade with large merchant vessels.

Meeting of the Senate usually took place in the Senate House in the Forum between dawn and dusk with the doors open so that the proceedings could be seen from without. It was rebuilt several times. In 50 BC Julius Caesar began rebuilding it after a fire in the previous year. His building was completed by Augustus, restored several times and finally rebuilt after AD 283 by Domitian. Other places such as temples could also be used for meetings if the Senate House was under repair.

The doors of the Curia were removed in 1660 and placed at the east end of the church of San Giovanni in Laterano. The first church was built by Constantine on the site of the barracks of the Equites Singulares, which he had disbanded in AD 312

Consuls presided over the proceedings and each senator spoke in order of rank, consuls and ex consuls taking precedence. Their role was to advise the magistrates on religious, domestic and foreign policy and they could vote on matters relating to these. Their authority stemmed from the fact that they were they were a permanent body with most men having personal knowledge and experience, especially on military, religious and political matters.

Under the empire the property qualification rose to over a million sesterces, which was intended to differentiate the senators from the equestrians. This resulted in the impoverishment of many of the old patrician families so that new senators were chosen, many though patronage by the emperor or by promotion from the provinces. The Senate still retained most of its powers of maintaining public order and conferring power on new emperors, which gave the appearance that it conferred legitimacy on them when many had come to power through action on the part of the army. Many senators were former governors of provinces so that their influence on policy could be considerable.

In the third century AD under the reforms of Diocletian and Constantine I their role declined as power and political and military offices were given to the equestrians. Constantine carried this policy further by enrolling equestrians into the ranks of senators and creating new posts for them in the army. By the end of his reign the number of senators had risen to 2000. This diluted their influence and experience, which became even less important when Constantine created a new Senate in Constantinople. As this also had a membership of 2000 it was clear that both houses might be considered mere 'talking shops' rather than effective governing bodies. Power now lay with the emperors and the office of senator implied status as a reward rather than status due to political power.

EQUESTRIANS

The equestrian order grew out of service with the cavalry. This, said to be about 300, later 1000 men, first served the kings, and was maintained theoretically by the state but practically was paid from property taxes raised on widows and orphans. Equestrians had to serve 10 campaigns and were given voting privileges in an assembly. In the fifth century BC men joined the *equites* paying their own way and bringing their own horses. Possibly these joined more for status than for an effective service because gradually equestrians were replaced by auxiliary troops, mostly drawn from the provinces.

The equestrians were not an intermediate class equivalent to a middle class. They strove as much as the patricians to gain wealth and to assert their power. As such they were appointed to official positions in the army and on governors' staffs. So many men from wealthy families began to join the order that in 129 BC senators were forbidden to join it and from then onwards the order became a distinct body. Successful businessmen and merchants from the provinces joined the order, the stipulation being that they had to be of free birth and hold some of their wealth in land. In that they were akin to senators and the two groups developed similar interests especially as the equestrians declared they were the social equals of senators and could marry into the patrician class. Some, because of their holding of magisterial offices could enter the Senate. Most, however, are believed to have pursued business interests rather than political power.

Augustus increased their influence by providing them with opportunities in financial administration. He created four boards of jurors from their ranks, each of 1000 men. Later Gaius added another board. These were honorary places that did not necessarily mean that they had to perform public duties. The order was now open to all freeborn men over the age of 18 having a wealth of 400,000 sesterces. Men often borrowed money or sought it from their patrons in order to gain admission. Pliny the Younger was pleased to give his friend Romatius Firmus, a town councillor of Comum, 300,000 sesterces 'for sound and serious reasons' to add to his capital to allow him to qualify for the order. After all, he said, they both came from the same town, went to the same school, had been friends since childhood and their families had always been friends. He added that 'an honourable position had to be maintained with special care if it was to keep alive the memory of a friend's generous gift.'

The equestrian rank was extremely popular in the provinces, especially for men living in towns and having wealth in land with a country villa. Special civil and military posts were open to them. They were distinguished by wearing a toga with a narrow stripe and had the right to have a horse paid for by the public purse. Augustus restored the right, which they had had in the early republic, of holding an annual parade on 15 July. Dionysius of Halicarnassus recorded seeing a procession of 5000 parading through Rome wearing decorations won in battle, crowned with olive leaves and attired in purple robes with scarlet stripes.

The main posts open to them were as equestrian officers in the army – prefects of infantry cohorts, military tribunes (at least one to each legion) and prefects of equestrian cavalry. Senior centurions could be created equestrians and move to higher ranks. From there they could be appointed to senior civil administrative positions, especially procurators in the provinces. Financial positions were popular, especially those with responsibility for the corn supply and posts in imperial palaces. Equestrians therefore mingled with the elite of the empire and could marry freely into senatorial families; indeed many sons of equestrians brought new blood into these. In the third century AD men who had served with distinction in the army became provincial governors and held high ranks in the legions. In fact by Domitian's reign most of these posts were held by equestrians and in the next century their progress had been so accelerated that their role had completely merged with that of senators.

MAGISTRATES AND THE CAREER STRUCTURE

The system of administration by magistrates was established during the republic. They were office holders elected for one year. So many applied for these positions that more than one person could hold an office at the same time. These offices were progressional so that an ambitious and conscientious man could follow a career path – the *cursus honorum*. There were a number of minor magistrates, young men elected for a year to do a particular job such as supervising cleaning of the city streets. This might be in preparation for the quaestorship. Others could be appointed to do a special job such as supervising prisons or keeping watch for fires.

A man began by being a quaestor. Two men, aged about 30, were elected each year, but as their duties increased more were required; eventually Sulla increased the number to 20, with each quaestor having different responsibilities. He also made the quaestorship a qualification for entering the Senate. Their main duties were to check taxation records and oversee financial

matters, especially those relating to letting out government contracts and paying contractors. In 48 BC Julius Caesar increased their number to 40.

The next step was to be elected an aedile. These men had to be 36 and were to supervise the city affairs. Their duties included monitoring markets, checking weights and measures and overseeing repairs to streets and roads. One onerous task was the burden of paying for public festivals and supervising these and festival games.

From there a man moved on to becoming a praetor about the age of 39. At first two men held the office but an increase in their duties meant that eight were appointed. Their task was to preside over some festivals, oversee the judiciary system – in particular the law courts – and undertake special tasks such as rooting out banditry. They were junior colleagues of the consul and could act for them if the consuls were away.

The last stage was to be elected as consul. Two consuls, aged over 40, were elected each year. Most of these men, at least during the republic, had served in the army so were conversant in both military and civil affairs. Their main duty was to see that public order was kept in Rome, receive embassies, lead discussion on foreign policy and prepare legislation. They might preside over certain aspects of law such as adoption and manumission.

Another office that could be part of the career structure was that of tribune. These men were appointed from the plebeians to look after their interests. They could propose legislation and check laws proposed by the Senate to see if they were to the detriment of the plebeians. They had the right of veto over such laws, could record actions of the officials and might overturn legal decisions. These actions could expose them to dangerous reprisals so they were given an unusual immunity from prosecution.

Each of these offices had a number of assistants called *lictors* attached to them, the number varying according to the office. As a symbol of the magistrates' power each lictor carried a *fasces*, an axe surrounded by a bundle of rods tied together with a purple ribbon. The symbolism was obvious. One rod could be broken but together they indicated the power and strength of the law. The axe indicated that the magistrates had the ultimate power to punish offenders with death.

In the republic election to these offices was made by groups of citizens. Consuls, praetors and censors were elected by the *comitia centuriata*. This was composed of groups called *centuries* which numbered 193. Voting by ballot on clay or stone tablets was introduced in 139 BC to ensure secrecy. The result accepted was by majority vote of each century. This seemingly democratic system was open to corruption by the fact that the majority of the wealthier citizens were distributed in the larger numbers of centuries compared to the number of poorer ones. Voting also did not take place at one time but by taking the votes of the wealthier citizens first. When the number of votes recorded reached 97 the voting was declared closed. Poor voters might therefore be deprived of having their votes recorded.

Aediles and quaestors in the republic were elected by the *comitia tributa*. For this the citizens were divided into tribes. In Rome there were four tribes within the city and 31 in the hinterland. Each tribe voted amongst itself and then the tribes cast a single vote. Thus 18 votes could win but the system was open to abuse for voters had to go to Rome to cast their votes directly, which meant that the wealthy, who might afford the time and the means to travel there, had the advantage.

The censors were not necessarily part of the career structure. They were appointed every five years to supervise the census and to consider the membership of citizens. Originally this had been one of the tasks of the consuls but they had often deputised this to their assistants. Censors were regarded as senior magistrates but had no legislative or judicial functions. They could have the duty of agreeing contracts for public works and account for taxes and rents and could farm out collection of these to the highest bidder. This could make them so open to bribes that censors were usually appointed from senators and after 209 bc from ex-consuls.

GOVERNMENT IN THE EMPIRE

It could be argued that Rome acquired an empire before she had an emperor. When Augustus assumed control Rome had already established provincial administrations in several areas including Sicily and Spain. More provinces were added during the empire, eventually numbering about 40. There were changes but the principle established was that there should be local self administration based on the administrative structure of Rome and taking into account as far as possible local traditions providing they did not contradict Roman law. As in the case of religion Rome was willing to tolerate a wide variety of local practices providing they were based on two considerations – the maintenance of public order and the efficient collection of taxes.

There were clearly certain differences. The first was that each province had a governor given power (*imperium*) first by the Senate and then by the emperor. It was impractical for a governor to hold office for only one year given the difficulty of establishing rapid communications with Rome. Many provinces had legions and auxiliary troops stationed in them and those governors had to be able to command authority with these armies. The republic therefore extended the *imperium* of the city magistrates to act in place of or on behalf of the consul or the praetor. Most governors had already held office as consul or praetor and were usually in place for two or three years.

When Augustus became emperor there were changes. The Senate was allowed to continue appointing governors to be proconsuls of Africa and Asia. Augustus took proconsular control of the provinces of Gaul, most of Spain, Syria, Cilicia, Cyprus and Egypt mainly because these were then areas where large numbers of troops were based. He appointed legates to command the troops but these were also governors. Augustus however held the *imperium* of a proconsul so his governors were appointed as *legati Augusti pro praetore*. This arrangement would apply to any area taken into the empire at a later date including Britain, Pannonia and Raetia. Emperors could choose men from the provinces to act as governors. Agricola, governor of Britain AD 78–84, was born in Gallia Narbonensis and might be considered a British specialist having served twice before in Britain as military tribune and, after his praetorship, as legate of the Twentieth Legion.

Usually senators were appointed but small provinces such as Raetia and Noricum, which could be troublesome, were given prefects appointed from the equestrian order. Judea with both nationalistic and religious problems also had an equestrian governor. These men were essentially military commanders and could be counted on to keep order. The Praefectus Aegypti of Egypt was a most important post, having proconsular military and civil power as he had to oversee the production of the grain supply which was essential to feed Rome.

Each governor was supplied with a staff of officials. In the republic the Senate appointed quaestors to be in charge of the finances of a province. Cicero was scathing of his quaestor when he was governor of Cilicia (51–50 BC) describing him as irresponsible, licentious and light-fingered. Collection of taxes was an important task, which could be farmed out to private companies (*publicani*) who had bought the right. Provinces were allocated a fixed sum in money or goods or both which had to be successfully transferred to Rome. A proportion could be kept to pay the expenses of the province and the army. Any surplus could be kept, hence the temptation for corrupt collusion between the quaestor and the *publicani*; if it was less it had to be made up. According to Suetonius, Tiberius said that it was the job of a good shepherd to shear his sheep not to skin them.

Governors received no salary but they had to have money for their expenses and could requisition corn for their staff. One of the first things Agricola did in Britain was to stop profiteering in the grain supply and stop abuses caused in its collection and distribution. A dishonest governor could make a profit on his governorship. Verres, after his governorship of Sicily (73–70 BC), was successfully prosecuted by Cicero for fraudulent dealings. Cicero was so careful in his management of the province that he handed back over two million sesterces which he had saved.

From the time of Augustus the quaestor in the imperial provinces was replaced by a procurator, who was directly responsible to the emperor. These could be useful sources of information as they could report on a governor's activities. They might abuse their powers as was seen in Britain when the rapacious tactics of the procurator, Decius Catus was partially responsible for the rising of the Trinovantes in the Boudiccan rebellion. It was also the reports sent by the next procurator, Julius Classicianus which forced the replacement of the governor Suetonius Paulinus who had taken severe repressive measures after that rebellion.

A governor could choose his own assistants who could have either military or civilian duties, but would also have the aid of professional civil servants. Pliny needed to have a considerable number of financial and legal experts when he was sent to Bithynia-Pontus. In addition the governor could invite a group of young men (*comites*) to go with him at his own expense. Careful checks had to be kept on these to see that they did not cause trouble. Tacitus made it clear that Agricola kept a firm discipline over his men. Cicero was accompanied as governor by his son and his nephew and also by a relative of his friend Atticus. He wrote to his brother Quintus that a good governor should take particular care in choosing his friends, as a governor has to answer for everything they do.

Governors in control of armies were not only responsible for their upkeep but also had to be able to lead them on campaigns. To men such as Agricola this was no problem but when Cicero was appointed as governor Cilicia he had last seen military action 32 years previously when he was 18. He was in charge of two legions in an area plagued by bandits and possibly facing invasion by the Parthians. Luckily they did not attack and Cicero managed to put down the bandits, capturing their stronghold at Pindenessus. He hoped in vain for the award of a triumph on his return to Rome but had to settle for being acclaimed as Imperator by his troops. Agricola, who might perhaps have deserved a triumph, avoided having one and was rewarded with a complimentary statue. It was Julius Caesar's extensive expansion of his territory during his governorship and his bravado in crossing Oceanus to invade Britain which led to his spectacular triumph.

Governors were also responsible for the law courts and for seeing that justice was administered correctly. Cicero was perhaps better at this task than at his military duties. If the governor was

not expert he could call on his staff to advise him in the *lex provinciae* which had been drawn up by a commission to apply especially to the provinces. He also had to settle disputes regarding citizenship and see that, if required, their cases were transferred to Rome.

Pliny's letters to Trajan from Bithynia indicated that he was concerned with regulating the finances of the town councils, overhauling the imperial post and ensuring justice. Much needed to be done. He wrote to Trajan bemoaning the fact that slaves who had been sentenced to service in the mines and the arena were now working as public slaves and getting a salary, yet if he stopped this practice they might become a burden on the state. Trajan gently reminded him: 'Let us not forget that the chief reason for sending you to your province was the evident need for reform.'

So conscientious was Pliny that when he sent his wife by the Imperial Post to visit her aunt because she had just had news of her grandfather's death, he informed the emperor but said that he felt sure that the emperor would approve of this because it was for family reasons. Trajan's reply showed his warmth for his friend and conscientious governor: 'You need not have any doubts even if you had waited to ask me if you could expedite your wife's journey by making use of these permits which I issued to you for official purposes. It is her duty to make her visit doubly welcome to her aunt by her prompt arrival.'

ROMAN INCORPORATION

During the empire more cities and towns were founded which were encouraged to establish councils with a magisterial system based on the model of those in Italy and in Rome itself. Aediles and quaestors were elected; *vigiles* were set up to fight fires. Law courts took account of Roman and local law. It was possible for men to acquire Roman citizenship and thereby promote themselves for office. By AD 212 when citizenship was extended to all peoples within the empire, it was assumed that these people would consider themselves part of one great empire and not inhabitants of a province attached to Rome. This was so taken for granted that it was possible for a man from a province, aided by men recruited from the provinces, to become emperor of Rome.

The great strength of Rome was its ability after conquering people to incorporate them into one great state, with a common language, where careers could be open to all men. Even if provincials might never be elected to the Roman Senate they could be elected to their own town councils and follow an urban career path which to some extent was modelled on that of Rome. Some men were accepted into the universal career structure, becoming governors of provinces or following careers within the imperial court. These men and their families were part of one empire, which until the barbarian invasions provided a stable system of government.

3

THE ECONOMY

Ancient Rome was a pre-industrial society. There were industries but these were small, using inefficient techniques. Also certain problems and attitudes prevented Rome developing both industry and agriculture. This is not to say that Rome did not establish a system of communications and industrial processes that to some extent suited her needs. Raw materials were available and Rome exploited the development of trading connections, ensuring that raw materials and finished commodities moved freely throughout the empire. Although this trading system was well-organised transporting goods was slow, expensive and often hazardous.

CARRIAGE OF GOODS

Carriage of goods by land was slow and cumbersome. Oxen were the chief traction animals; mules and donkeys were pack animals but carriage of goods was limited by how much could be placed in their panniers. A team of oxen might shift marble columns for public buildings when paid for by the state, but this required about 30 oxen to pull one large drum. A padded collar was not invented until the Middle Ages. The Romans harnessed animals either by a yoke over the horns or by a broad band over the breastbone of the animal. Unfortunately this tended to rise and throttle the animal as it pressed on the windpipe. It was far cheaper to transport goods by water but this required the originating place and the receiving place to be near water; hence many of the most flourishing Roman cities were on the banks of a navigable river. One problem was that although large rivers were navigable throughout the year, others might flood in winter and have low water during the summer.

The Romans did build some canals. One such is the Car Dyke in the Fen area of Britain running from near Cambridge to Lincoln; another, the Fossdyke, enabled barges to move from Lincoln to the navigable River Trent. There was always a problem of cost. Governor of Bithynia Pliny wrote to Trajan with a suggestion to join Lake Sophon to the sea by a canal, 29km (18 miles) long, because although 'marble, farm produce, wood and timber for building are easily and cheaply brought by boat, they then have to be taken on to the sea by cart with great

difficulty and increased expense.' To build this canal 'would require a great deal of labour, but there was no lack of this' and, he added hopefully, people in countryside and town 'will all gladly help with a scheme which will benefit them all.' Trajan, who obviously did not wish to crush Pliny's enthusiasm, answered that they must first make an accurate survey and he suggested Pliny applied to Calpurnius Macer, (Legate of Lower Moesia AD 111–112) for an engineer.

SOURCES OF POWER

One particular problem lay in the sources of power. The Romans relied on human and animal power to perform normal working practices. A slave economy encouraged this but it could result in low average productivity of labour. A man driving an ox plough does not have the same productive capacity as a man driving a tractor. There were some advances in technology. The Romans developed watermills in the first century AD to grind their grain; one at Barbegal near Arles was a complex arrangement of 16 water wheels set in pairs built down a steep hillside to take advantage of the flow of water, which was an advance on slaves or donkeys turning a hopper. This may have ground 300kg (660lbs) of grain an hour. Roman water wheels still exist at Hama in Syria. Rome had several water powered mills including one using water from the Aqua Traiana on the Janiculum.

By the end of the fourth century AD watermills drove power saws. Ausonius spoke of a stream turning 'the millstones round and round with savage force driving the shrieking saws through smooth blocks of marble.' The Romans were aware of the practices of compressed air and steam. Mechanical devices were used to promote greater productivity, the screw press

Section of a waterwheel from the Rio Tinto mines, Spain. Eight pairs of wheels could raise water up 59.5m (97ft). (British Museum)

Relief showing a reaping machine.
(Institute Archéologique de
Luxembourg, Arlon, Belgium)

increased the yield from pressing olives and grapes, the screw pump lifted water out of rivers and huge water wheels cleared water from the silver mines of Spain. But these inventions were not exploited. Simple improvements were adopted, the scythe replaced the sickle, thus increasing the rate of cutting grain, and a more efficient plough with a coulter which turned the sod, but a mechanical reaper mentioned by Pliny the Elder and seemingly illustrated on a relief at Arlon (Belgium) does not seem to have been developed.

There were also advances in industrial processes such as glass making and building crafts but these relied on human labour rather than the development of an advanced technology. Petronius satirises a man who approached Tiberius for a reward for inventing unbreakable glass. Tiberius asked him if he had told anyone else his secret and when he was assured that the man had not, promptly had him executed, adding dryly 'Gold should not be reduced to the value of mud.' Larger industries such as mining and quarrying were run by the state or leased out to individuals under imperial control; both used criminals and slaves as cheap and expendable labour. Other industries relied on craftsmen, often freedmen, who had learned a trade after manumission. These organised themselves into guilds, not to promote their businesses collectively or improve working practices, but to provide meeting places for convivial dinners and acting as burial clubs to ensure that the correct rites were performed at death.

Almost all manufacturing processes relied on work being carried out by hand and took place in small workshops or in households. Large workshops which relied on high productivity such as the pottery industry could make some gestures towards the division of labour – one man producing a pot and another decorating it, a third packing it – but the quality of the finished products could and did vary enormously.

The Roman aqueduct at Segovia, Spain, built in the reign of Augustus, consists of 128 double arches and shows how Roman engineers supported one arch above another. It stands 27.4m (90ft) at its highest point and still carries a water supply across the valley

PREJUDICE

Possibly the main reason for the lack of industrial development was lack of will and prejudice against it by those who had the wealth to push the boundaries. This attitude extended to minor officials whose duty was to understand the immediate process and keep services in good order, not to have an inventive attitude, except where a more efficient service could be obtained. Aristotle had stressed that in no well-ordered state could an artisan be a citizen with full civic rights. The life of the intellect was superior to a life of toil. Cicero made a clear distinction between those who were gentlemen (doctors, architects, teachers) and those who were vulgar and these included workmen 'whose very wages are the pledges of slavery, those who buy from wholesale merchants in order to retail immediately, and all mechanics, for no workshop can have anything liberal about it.'

This prejudice extended to ploughing profits back into a business. Wealth was to be used to promote a career, to satisfy clients and to provide public buildings, which would leave a legacy reflecting on a man's position in life. Wealth from industry was to be despised. Wealth was acceptable if it came from booty gained in war or from landed estates supervised by a bailiff and probably owned by an urban landowner. Cato and Columella give copious notes on farming and farming methods without once mentioning growing surpluses and exploiting farms for profit. Cato praised the farming class by which he meant the gentleman farmer whose farm was run by a bailiff as being the class from which the 'bravest men and the sturdiest soldiers came, their calling is the most highly respected.'

Farming manuals give detailed instructions as to the duties of a bailiff and his wife particularly in their treatment of the slaves. If a bailiff was not required land could be rented out. Tenant farmers were particularly important as they provided a solution to the problem of an owner working an estate distant from his usual home, and which he visited infrequently. There was always a risk that the tenant might neglect the property or not be able to pay his rent, or that the owner might dismiss the tenant at short notice. Therefore the system came to be carefully regulated in Roman law.

A number of writers discussed theories of technological processes although some of these seem bizarre, for example the devices used to mesmerize the beholders when they enter a temple, but many books were practical handbooks. Frontinus's book *De Aquis Urbis Romae* is a straightforward account of the aqueducts, their history, the rules governing them and details regarding the distribution of water. These included trenches to take the water lined with wooden piles enclosing stone blocks along the line of the trench to support a stone roof or over ground arches supporting a water channel, but there is a suspicion that it was written to demonstrate Frontinus's capacity for administration. Military manuals (Vegetius) and architectural treatises (Vitruvius) were used as handbooks by professionals but most writers deemed it more appropriate to discuss the theory of law, politics and the liberal arts.

ENGINEERING

The army with its technical strength produced excellent engineers. The public often depended on their military efficiency, especially their skilled craftsmen. From the reign of Hadrian when

Metal sheaths from the bases of piles of Caesar's bridge crossing the Rhine. (Rheinisches Museum, Bonn)

Relief from the tomb of the Haterii. On the left slaves are crowding into the treadmill of the crane which is being used to build the temple on the right. At the top a deceased woman lies on her deathbed, surrounded by her retainers

legions were more settled in their provinces they undertook more civil tasks and by the time of Probus in the third century AD the army often built bridges, colonnades temples and other public works in cities.

It would be wrong to say that there were no great achievements in engineering. The Romans built a road system, which lasted long after the end of their empire. Rivers were crossed by bridges, many forming the basis of those in use today. The bridge across the Danube for the Roman army, built in AD 104 by Apollodorus, was 1127.7m (3700ft) long and 12.2–10.6m (40–35ft) wide. Builders were able to transport heavy loads of construction material, and on site raise huge blocks by means of block and tackle and pulley and windlass. The tomb relief of the Haterii shows a crane being constructed with a large treadmill wheel in which slaves are scrabbling to turn it. By this means the Romans were able to raise blocks necessary to create magnificent buildings and monuments and, as they had invented a means of supporting an arch and one arch rising above another, they could construct buildings, and aqueducts with a calculated water flow, to great height. They invented a strong building cement incorporating quicklime, broken stone and pebbles, which supported these huge monuments. These were achieved in spite of the awkward system of numbers, which meant that a simple arithmetical calculation could be difficult. They made no use of trigonometry.

AGRICULTURE

The economy depended greatly on the use made of land, in particular cultivated land, which could produce food. Such land is a finite resource. Not only is there a limit to the amount of fertile, productive land but also there is a limit to the productivity of that land if it is not cultivated correctly. As production expanded so less fertile land was brought into cultivation and attempts were made to produce greater yields. But expansion of agriculture into marginal lands might be at the expense of other activities such as herding and hunting. The Romans had developed a form of crop rotation but were often forced to leave land fallow every two years, in spite of trying different methods of rotation, thus cutting down on crop yields. Manuring would help – animal manure, human excrement, pigeon dung and clay marling; olive oil dregs were placed around trees. Winter wheat needed rich soil and so was sown every second year. Barley was sown in very rich or very poor soil as the Roman agricultural writer Columella suggested 'the land is weakened by this crop'. Beans and other pulses could be planted in rich soil between crops of wheat and barley. Roman writers stressed the value of vines and olive trees. Those, together with grain and vegetables, would allow a farm to become almost self-supporting. Columella recommended growing wheat between olive trees because the trees bear a crop only in alternate years.

Increasing the labour supply meant more mouths to feed and it was not only people in the country who had to be fed. The aim was self-sufficiency. A farm might produce enough food to feed its inhabitants with some surplus to take to a nearby market, as the peasant Simulus intends to do in the poem *Moretum*. The expansion of towns meant that a non-productive number of people had also to be fed and this might require the produce of 10 farms to feed one non-productive family.

To minimise the risk of crops failing landowners preferred to have a number of scattered holdings rather than concentrate on one large farm holding. Cato stated that landowners should not make investments in large farms, agreeing with Virgil that it is best to admire these but keep a small one. He recommended a 'hundred *iugera*' about 0.27 hectares (two-thirds of an acre). Landowners grew a large variety of crops so that at least some would survive. This might minimise the risk but it did increase the amount of labour required and limit the amount of surplus production. The system also militated against a huge surplus cash crop that could be sold in bulk.

Land, however, meant wealth and the acquisition of it became a priority. Ownership, be it that of a peasant farmer or an aristocrat of great estates, satisfied a need to be part of country life, to get back to rural roots. Most of the descriptions of country life, as in Virgil's *Georgics*, extolled its virtues with more than a little poetic licence, but the practical manuals of Cato, Varro, Columella and Palladius were intended to help farmers and estate owners. Varro wrote his manual when he was in his eighties as a guide for his younger wife who had just bought a property. His advice, however, could be useful to any estate owner. Pliny the Elder's encyclopaedic *Natural History* described plant, animal and inanimate forms. There could be a problem, however, if an ambitious man wished to increase his surplus or invest in larger properties for he might become liable to higher taxation. All agricultural land was taxed so the best use had to be made of it. Landowners had to supply the army with grain, hides and produce or the tax collector with cash.

Another problem was inheritance laws, which insisted that fathers must provide for sons. Splitting the land could mean the eldest sons had the largest portion so that younger sons had little land and therefore had to find themselves new jobs or properties. Many joined the army thus proving a ready supply of manpower. But the empire produced another solution – conquest meant acquiring new lands, which at first became state owned land (*ager publicus*). This remorseless expansion of Rome from the late republic period until the second century AD allowed land to be taken over and bought by or given to the ambitious. Soldiers were settled in *coloniae* and given land after 25 years service. This provided a solution to the problems of retiring veterans and also ensured that the concept of Romanisation was part of political policy in most parts of the empire.

PROBLEMS OF EXPANSION

The expansion of Rome distorted trading conditions, for Roman conquest could be disastrous for other areas. Much of their wealth and often their manpower were diverted to Rome leaving some regions impoverished; others depended on Rome rather than native talent. Two demands in particular resulted from this. One was the demands of the army. Not all provinces housed huge numbers of legionaries and auxiliaries. Those that did such as Britain, the Danube and Rhine frontiers might be the least productive. The army, although a source of craftsmen, engineers and other talent, lacked basic commodities which had to be sought locally or supplied by long distance trade. In Britain local supplies of grain, pottery and leather seem to have been obtained and in the fourth century, the Emperor Julian was able to commandeer sufficient supplies of grain from Britain to provide for his army in the Rhineland. Frontier regions in the

eastern provinces, however, required major imports to support them, especially food for the men and fodder for animals. The army also needed huge quantities of leather and metal. The provinces had to be taxed heavily to supply these.

The other demand came from the city of Rome itself. By the beginning of the empire its population had reached about a million and it continued to grow. These people had to be fed and housed. They had to be entertained and impressed. Emperors wished to indicate their personal largess and leave their mark on the city. Building projects needed huge amounts of building material – marble from Egypt, Greece and Asia Minor, minerals from Britain, Dacia and Spain. North Africa was almost denuded of wild animals to provide entertainment in the amphitheatres. Wine, olive oil and especially grain was needed, for this was often distributed freely by the emperors. First Sicily and then Egypt became the grain baskets of Rome. *Negotiatores* were responsible for moving grain to Ostia, where it was stored in great granaries before transfer along the Tiber to Rome and into other warehouses around the area of the Aventine.

Regular distribution of grain had begun when Sicily, Africa and Sardinia paid taxes to Rome in the form of grain. Monthly sales of cut-price grain to free-born citizens had begun in 123 BC arranged by the Tribune of the Plebs, Gaius Gracchus, who built large granaries to hold the supply. Some patricians objected as they wished to dispense grain to their own clients or as a charitable gift to freedmen and slaves to enhance their popularity. Augustus wanted to abolish the grain dole but bowed to necessity and added Egypt to the suppliers of grain and established an office of Prefect of Grain Supplies to organise provision for the city. A good

A man filling a corn measure levels the grain with a rod. Mosaic in the Square of the Corporations, Ostia

supply had to be available for Rome's population and in the empire it was distributed for free to the poor. Garnsey estimated that if Rome had a million inhabitants, each of them required at least 200kg (440lbs) of grain each year and that the Romans needed to import between 120,000 and 400,000 tonnes of grain yearly in order to satisfy the population. Antoninus Pius added free pork and wine for those entitled to a grain ration and Septimius Severus ordered distributions of free oil to the poor.

Claudius was adamant that inducements had to be made to ensure traders had the ships to transport the grain. He granted privileges to any shipper who could guarantee to supply shiploads of grain of at least 10,000 *modii* (70 tonnes) of grain for six years and rebuilt the enclosed harbour, which Julius Caesar had originally planned, two miles north of Ostia and linked it to the Tiber by a canal. This became unusable if there were fierce gales, so Trajan built an inner basin at Portus. Occasionally the grain supply broke down as happened in AD 99 when the Nile did not flood enough to fertilise sufficient agricultural land, and Trajan had to order the ships coming from Egypt to return there to provide the basic needs of that province.

Rome also attracted other groups of people. Artists, sculptors and craftsmen came from Greece and Asia Minor; teachers arrived from Greece and Egypt. According to Livy cooks made their way to Rome from Greece and Asia Minor after 189 BC, a specific date relating to Gnaeus Manlius Vulso bringing back some after his campaign in Galatia. Slaves brought to Rome could be manumitted, becoming freedmen and setting up their own businesses. Merchants or *negotiatores* supplied goods for the city and there was always a ready market. Rome had a daily retail market by 210 BC and later a wholesale market, the Emporium. Both the Forum Boarium and the Forum Holitorium became important commercial areas and Trajan's huge market complex in AD 113, an adjunct to his forum, supplied the retail trade.

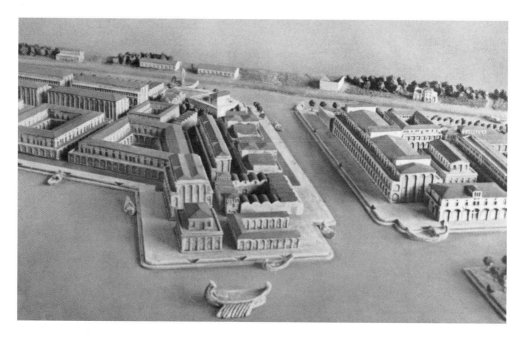

Model of Trajan's harbour at Ostia

TRADE

Many wealthy Romans refused or were reluctant to become associated with trade because of the risks this could entail and also because it was beneath their social status. This allowed opportunities for the middleman to become involved, making contracts with the landowners to market or export their goods. *Negotiatores*, whose activities were controlled by law, were involved in a vast number of activities. They carried out business deals and would supply manpower to an estate, such as that needed for picking and pressing grapes at the harvest. Many were equestrians; others were wealthy freedmen. They were usually based in Rome or in the major ports where they used their connections with overseas markets to promote trade, set up deals and see that they were completed. This was particularly important in dealing with shippers and with merchants who wished to hire part of the space in a ship for their cargoes. Many deals would have collapsed without their aid. This went beyond trading matters for they were useful in securing land, collecting taxes and even loaning cash. By the first century AD they were specialising so that inscriptions record a dealer in oil (*negotiator olearius*) and a dealer in wine (*negotiator vinarius*).

In particular they supplied Rome with luxury goods. Ivory was used for carved figures and inlay for furniture. Gold and silver was needed for jewellery, tableware, religious objects and statue decoration. Silver was rare in Rome until the Second Punic War when rich resources were opened up in Spain. Silver dishes were particularly welcome as presents for emperors and were given by clients to patrons in the hope of advancement. There was a well-established trade in furs from northern Europe and amber from the Baltic. About AD 166 Roman merchants reached the Han capital in China, thus sealing Rome's contact with the east. Silk was brought from China and wild silk from India. Spices, especially pepper, flowed into Rome from China and India, together with ivory, pearls, gemstones and silk. Even oysters were brought from Britain.

Spices were particularly welcome and a great advance in long distance trade was made during Claudius's reign when a Greek merchant Hippalus, who sailed from the Red Sea to the Indian Ocean, elucidated the wind system of the monsoon. An unknown writer in the first century AD published *The Periplus of the Erythraean Sea* detailing the harbours, sea conditions and safest routes to the East. As the south-west monsoon prevailed from April to October and the north-east from October to April it became possible to sail from the Egyptian port of Berenice to Calicut in India in 70 days, and to make the return journey within the year. Ships would leave port in July and use the winds to reach the mouth of the Ganges or the Malabar Coast in south India, and then return in November. Their cargo would be transferred overland to Alexandria and other ports for shipment to Rome from whence it would be distributed. The discovery of the route reduced the dependency of Rome on the Arabian overland route. The spice trade increased enormously and Rome became the distribution centre for the empire.

The eastern trade was extremely lucrative although some Romans regarded its expansion as disastrous, corrupting and weakening republican virtues. Seneca railed against luxurious banquets and elaborate dress, describing them as 'diseases against the state'. However, not all the luxury trade was unnecessary as far as some sections of the population were concerned; incense was needed for ritual purposes and spices for cooking and medicine. Growth in demand was also vital for the economy.

The vast array of local goods on sale in Rome and elsewhere is summed up by Cato when detailing where a farmer or villa owner might obtain his goods:

> Tunics, togas, blankets, smocks and shoes should be bought at Rome; caps, iron tools, scythes, spades, mattocks, axes, harness, ornaments, and small chains at Cales and Minturnae; spades at Venafrum; carts and sledges at Suessa and in Lucania; jars and pots at Alba and Rome; and tiles at Venafrum. Roman yokes are the best made. The following cities are the best markets for the articles named: oil mills at Pompeii, and at Rufrius's yard at Nola; nails and bars at Rome; pails, oil-urns, water pitchers, other copper vessels at Capua and Nola; Campanian buckets from Capua will be found useful; pulley ropes and all sorts of cordage at Capua; Roman baskets at Suessa and Casinum.

For international trade the words of the Revelation of St John the Divine believed to date from the end of the first century AD can suffice to sum up the products of Rome:

> And the merchants of the earth shall weep and mourn over her; for no man buyeth their merchandise any more: the merchandise of gold and silver and precious stones and of pearls and fine linen, and purple and silk and scarlet, all thyngs wood, and all manner of vessels of ivory; vessels of precious wood and of brass, iron and marble. And cinnamon, spices, ointments, frankincense, wine, oil, fine flour and wheat, and beasts, sheep, horses and chariots and slaves and the souls of men.

COINAGE

Coins had first been produced in the Greek cities of Asia Minor in the late seventh century BC and these soon spread throughout the Aegean. Coinage reached the Greek colonies of southern Italy about 500 BC. In much of Italy at that time currency was in the form of irregular bronze lumps, which had a value according to the weight of each piece. By the third century BC these lumps had been divided into a series of weights, many stamped with the name of Rome.

This was not considered an efficient system so by about 290 BC bronze pieces of up to 100mm (4in) in diameter were produced. One of these was called an *as* (plural *asses*) but they were inconvenient as they weighed about one Roman pound (324g, 11.5oz). They were therefore divided into lesser weights: the *semi* (half-*as*), the *triens* (a third), the *quadrans* (quarter), the *sextans* (sixth) and the *uncia* (ounce).

Later silver coins were produced based on Greek coins. A silver *denarius* was produced about 211 BC (equal to 10 *asses*) and this remained the main coin until the third century AD. Gradually the *as* was reduced in size and adjustments made to the others until a reasonable coinage emerged. Towards the end of the second century BC the *sestertius* was produced, equal to a quarter of a denarius.

Gold is always regarded as the most prestigious of metals so it is not surprising that gold coins called *staters* were produced in Rome during the Second Punic War and successful generals began to produce them to pay their own armies. Not all of them could be valued at their true worth, those of Mark Anthony being seriously debased. Augustus was determined

to establish an efficient and trustworthy system and therefore issued a new coinage based on four metals, gold silver, brass and bronze. Gold and silver alone were to be used for official salaries; the other two were for loose change. Augustus did not completely rule out the use of local currency in the provinces, which continued to be used. He was determined, however, to establish one Roman monetary unit throughout the empire. In theory only the emperor had the right to issue gold coins but in practice he allowed other mints to strike them and in their own style. Antioch, Alexandria and Rhodes therefore continued to produce *drachmas* and *tetradrachmas*. He allowed the Senate to produce bronze coins, and also cities in other parts of the empire, provided they were stamped with his image. Later other cities in the provinces were allowed to establish mints and produce coins provided they followed those struck in Rome.

The coinage was based in accordance with the bullion weight of the gold *aureus*. A silver *denarius* was a quarter of this; a bronze *sestertius* was a hundredth part or four *asses* and a *dupondius* a two-hundredth part or two asses. Below these came the *as*, the *semi* and the *quadrans*. As the last two were equal in monetary value to 800 and 1000 parts of an *aureus* they soon disappeared from circulation. The *sestertius* retained its importance, as did the *denarius* until the debasement of the coinage by Septimius Severus meant that it became more a bronze than a silver coin.

This system of coinage remained until the reign of Caracalla when a new coin, the *antoninianus* (Antonine), was introduced in debased silver. Debasement of the coinage continued and several attempts at currency reform were attempted by Aurelian. When Britain and Gaul broke from Rome and formed the ill-fated Gallic Empire in the third century, they issued coins of poor quality that had local circulation. Further reform therefore had to come from Diocletian and Constantine, but there was constant alteration of the coinage until the end of the empire.

BANKING OPERATIONS

Large payments were made in hard cash by banking operations, which were carried out in Rome by the *argentarii*, whose shops were near and round about the Forum, and by the *nummulaii* who tested and exchanged money. Both these groups were controlled by the state, especially as valuables and money could be entrusted to them. They were allowed to charge interest, usually 6–10 per cent. This system soon spread throughout the empire but in the provinces much money had to be borrowed to pay taxes leading to enormous debts. Wealthy Romans would also agree to lend money but during the first century AD this often confused the native population. It was the calling in of such loans in AD 60, because of Roman unease about the unrest in Britain, which was partially responsible for the support given by the Trinovantian tribe to the Boudiccan rebellion.

UNIFORMITY OF WEIGHTS AND MEASURES

Currency reform helped to unify the Roman world, as did a system of weights and measures. Measures of length were based mainly on parts of the human body, the normal Roman foot

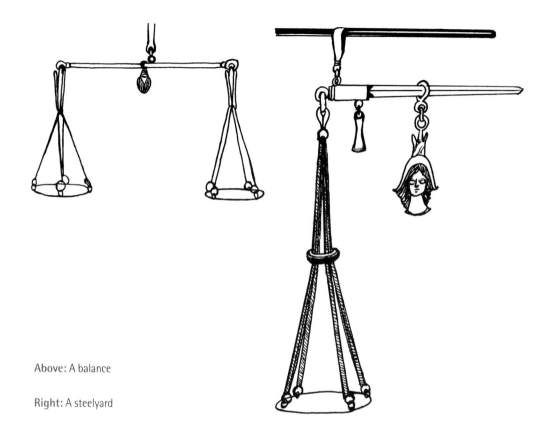

Above: A balance

Right: A steelyard

being about 296mm (11.65in). For measuring distances the pace was used, one pace being five Roman feet.

Measures of capacity were based on wet measures of wine and olive oil and dry measures of grain. The last was placed in a bronze bucket-shaped vessel (*modius*), which had the capacity marked on the side. Measures of weight were based on the pound (*libra*) and the ounce (*uncia*). Two forms of balance were used. One had two scale pans dangling by chains from opposite end of a rod. Goods were put into one pan and lead, bronze or stone weights into the other. Correct weight meant that the two should balance. The other was the steelyard where goods to be weighed were placed in one pan or attached by a hook linked by chains to one horizontal arm. A weight was moved along this arm until it balanced the other arm. The weight of the goods was measured by marks on the horizontal arm.

4

HOUSING AND THE HOUSEHOLD

Within the Roman Empire there was a wide variety of housing with each province developing its own style often based on local tradition but with some interjection of the classical tradition. Houses would also vary in size and appearance according to individuals' wealth and status and whether they lived in the town or the country. For the wealthy they represented their status in life and often acted as an office; for the lower classes they reflected what they were but improvement was an aspiration and a social ambition.

Information on housing in Rome is mainly gathered from Roman writers. Three other towns in Italy provide evidence through actual remains: Pompeii and Herculaneum, excavated from the destruction caused by the eruption of Vesuvius in AD 79, and Ostia, which was gradually deserted as its importance declined when the Tiber mouth silted up. Pompeii, which was not strictly a Roman town but a colony created in 80 BC after its defeat in the Social Wars, had received Hellenistic influence through contact with Greek merchants and social and architectural practices from central Italy. It therefore had a different identity from Rome. Ostia, the port of Rome, was subject to much more Roman influence with the majority of the population being engaged in industries and businesses connected with shipping.

APARTMENT BLOCKS

In Rome the vast majority of the population lived in tenement blocks often five to six storeys high. Augustus had set a height of 21m (70ft). Trajan lowered it to 18.3m (60ft). This height could have resulted in four storeys of average height 3.5m (11.5ft) and a fifth somewhat lower. These types of buildings had existed in Rome since the third century BC and reflected the Roman model of using space economically. These often covered a single block (*insula*) and usually consisted of four wings built round a central courtyard. They could be divided into apartments comprising single rooms or two to five rooms rented to one family linked by a corridor. Wealthy tenants, who could be charged higher rents, probably lived on the lower floors.

Tenants had to reach their apartments by crumbling staircases. Martial, who lived in such a block before he moved to Spain, satirised Satra, 'the most miserly and greedy of men', who after a huge meal carried off the leftovers and the dregs of wine before climbing up 200 stairs and shutting himself in his room. His foresight in obtaining this food may have been because he had no kitchen. There was too great a danger of fire. Tenants might cook on a brazier but food could be bought from street sellers and food establishments. Shops on the ground floor might have a mezzanine floor for storage of goods or as living quarters. These could be accessed either from the shop or from a stair in the courtyard.

Residents included craftsmen and tradesmen, professional people and younger sons from aristocratic households who wanted more freedom. Rapacious landlords, speculative builders or wealthy Romans might own the block. Cicero owned several *insulae*. In April 44 BC he wrote to Atticus that in one *insula* two shops had collapsed and other parts of the building were showing cracks so that the mice had moved elsewhere to say nothing of the tenants. He added that people might call it a disaster but he did not even call it a nuisance. There was a building scheme under way which should turn his loss into a profit. Building and repair work were always taking place. Juvenal said sarcastically that 'We inhabit a Rome for the most part supported by props.' This was how an agent stopped buildings from falling down so tenants did not have to worry about the cracks.

The people in these apartment blocks would have had little furniture. Juvenal satirised Cordus who lived in an upper storey of an apartment block, which caught fire. He was too late to save his pitiable possessions – a small bed, six jugs, a cupboard, an earthenware statue of a centaur and a box in which he kept his Greek books. No one would give him food and shelter when he was naked or begging for scraps. Martial said that a poor man had a toga, a bug-ridden bed, a rush mat, a key and cup. When Martial's Vacerra does a moonlight flit he takes his bed, table, lantern and wooden bowl. Poor people had few possessions but that made them the more dearly missed if they were lost or stolen.

Few blocks have been discovered in Rome. One was unearthed beneath the Galleria Colonna on the eastern side of the Via del Corso. Another, built in the second century AD alongside the Capitoline Hill, rose to six storeys and had shops on the ground floor with porticoes demanded by Nero's regulations. The third storey had three apartments and those above had rows of single rooms leading off corridors, but overcrowding was so common that people probably squeezed themselves into any niche they could find or lived in the corridors. Other blocks have been incorporated into later buildings. Several blocks have survived at Ostia. One, the so-called Casa di Diana built as part of a huge development during Trajan's reign probably to house an increasing population, now only has three storeys, but obviously rose higher. It probably housed about 40 or more people. Access was provided to the upper storeys by staircases entered directly from the street constructed in stone or by wooden treads on bricks. The main light in the corridors came from the street or the courtyard. Windows had wooden shutters, as glass was too expensive. Water could not be piped to the upper floor so it had to be collected from a fountain and basin in the courtyard. There were no individual latrines except for a communal one on the ground floor. For daily use there were always public latrines or those in the public baths.

The Casa di Diana, Ostia, had shops on the ground floor and a balcony, which may have been a decorative feature, on the third floor

The Ostia apartments are of brick with no cement or stucco decoration. Vitruvius said that the best brick was that which had been sun-baked for two years, but few builders could wait that long. Earlier apartments at Ostia might have been built of timber, as were many of those in Rome. The entrances are framed with pilasters. Balconies are added on the street side, but they were not true balconies because they were not accessible from within. Some were of wood supported on corbels. The thickness of the walls – 59cm (23 in) – would bear the weight of five storeys. Windows were small and barred by grilles or heavy shutters. Most interior walls were bare; some were plastered. The roof of the building was probably of tiles supported on wooden beams – flat tiles with round edges alternately placed with semi-cylindrical ties. Decorative slabs, cornices and antefixes protected the ends of wooden beams. Terracotta antefixes could be very decorative. Two apartment blocks found at Herculaneum had frontages of 80m (262ft) and rose to a height of 12.2m (40ft), possibly higher, but any upper storeys were destroyed in the volcanic eruption. The ground floor had shops or even an inn. The upper storeys were reached by wooden staircases.

A relief found at Lake Furcino near Avezzano, Italy, dated to AD 213 showing a town surrounded by a wall. The streets are laid out in a grid pattern

Fire was a constant hazard, hence Augustus's creation of the *vigiles*. Juvenal commented that 'We detest fires' and spoke sarcastically that if fires began on the ground floor the occupants might be shouting for water and getting their belongings out while those on the third floor, oblivious to the noise would be the last to burn. The only way to control fires was to pull down the buildings in the path of the fire, but inhabitants, regardless of the danger to their neighbours, would try to prevent this. After the fire of AD 64 Nero ordered a space of 3m (10ft) to be left between blocks, and porticos were built along facades to aid fire fighters to reach further up buildings. These narrow streets can be appreciated in a relief found at Lake Nemi dating from the first century AD. This depicts part of a Roman town set within a massive wall with the two- or three-storey buildings packed together.

Noise was a great nuisance. Martial said that bakers disturbed people at night and coppersmiths hammered all day. Seneca who lived above a set of public baths complained of the noise of bathers and the screams of those who were having hair plucked from their armpits. Juvenal commented that in Rome many invalids died from insomnia and you had to be very

A fountain and street in Pompeii

rich to sleep in that city. Traffic rumbled through the streets and drivers swore as they drove their herds to market. The noise and bustle during day and night was constant, echoing off the narrow streets. Juvenal mentioned tiles crashing off the roofs and the contents of chamber pots being poured from upper storey windows. Much of this noise was due to life being lived in the open as people moved out to escape their small and smelly rooms, to enjoy company and just sit around. Seneca spoke of people wandering about houses and theatres, in the forum, meddling and interested in public affairs, always curious to see what was happening. They might gawp at a funeral, watch a wedding or attend a trial. They would even walk behind a litter in the hope of carrying it. Horace and Juvenal spoke of the difficulty in forcing a way through crowds and avoiding ruffians' angry curses. Soldiers stood on toes in their hobnailed boots and, even worse, carts carrying marble could overturn and crush people.

WEALTHIER HOUSING

There were better houses for the wealthy and most of the evidence for these can be seen in Pompeii and Herculaneum. These were single or double storey houses consisting of rooms placed round courtyards and atriums. The house looked inwards. The outer walls facing the street were blank, painted red or had some stucco decoration. Their blank nature, however, attracted posters and graffiti, especially during elections. Small windows were set high up for security. The entrance was usually tall with huge wooden doors which had large locks. On either side might be shops; the House of Sallust at Pompeii had a bar in its frontage. A corridor led into the atrium past porters' lodges or seats on which clients waited for their patron's attention. Corridors had mosaic floors; the House of Paquius Proculus had a chained dog, the House of the Tragic Poet's chained dog added the words 'Cave Canem'.

The main rooms of the house, the dining room (*triclinium*) and the day room (*tablinum*) could separate the atrium from a smaller courtyard (*peristyle*) that opened onto a garden. Bedrooms, reception and recreation rooms occupied one or both sides of the atrium. There could be considerable variation in the layout of the houses. Wealthy householders wished to show their largess so visitors could be received in the atrium, seen from the entrance, where statues and other decorative arts would be on view. This could be a women's workroom or a children's play area in the afternoon. Visitors might be received in the *tablinum* which would give views of both the atrium and the *triclinium* or the *peristyle*. The upper storey would contain bedrooms and store rooms.

Pompeian houses had elaborate decorated rooms with frescoes in a variety of artistic styles – architectural features, painted effects, flower and plant vegetation, mythological scenes and those relating to real life. Many of the floors had geometrical or figured mosaics often strategically placed so that they could be admired. Gardens would be laid out with paths and fountains and a variety of plants. Important *lararia* were placed in the atrium or the *triclinium*, the latter so that the Lares could preside over the food.

Many houses had private latrines and some had baths, although the public baths provided social activity as well as a means to keep clean. Latrines, placed in small courtyards or near kitchens, had two or four places with wooden seats or a wooden board fixed on two bricks. In a latrine at the House of the Gem at Herculaneum was the graffiti '*Apollinaris medicus Titi*

A mosaic from the entrance of the House of the Tragic Poet showing a chained dog and the words Cave Canem (Beware of the dog)

imperatoris hic cacavit bene': 'Apollinaris, a physician to the emperor Titus, had a good shit here.' People wiped themselves with sponges on sticks, pieces of cloth or leaves. Cesspits were cleared out by slaves who also brought water for sluicing down the latrines. In addition, lower parts of dolia or amphorae would be placed in the kitchen, and strategically at street corners, so that urine could be collected for use in the tanning industry. Many Pompeian houses were connected to water mains by means of lead piping. These did not necessarily connect to the kitchen but were used to feed fountains and garden pools. Slaves would collect buckets of water for use in the kitchen.

In Pompeii and Herculaneum kitchens can often be identified by a *lararium* placed so the Lares could supervise the cooking arrangements, or by a raised hearth set against the wall and edged with a curb to hold in hot charcoal. On this would be placed tripods and gridirons. A square or semi-circular base at the bottom held fuel. There might also be a large brick oven. Kitchens were placed away from the main house because of the danger of fire. Cooking or heating of food bought from the numerous cooking establishments could also be done on portable braziers.

A reconstructed kitchen hearth with cooking pans in the Museo Archeologico Nazionale, Naples, based on that found in the House of the Vettii

Lararium in the kitchen of the House of the Dancing Fawn. This would have held small figurines, probably including a pair of Lars and a Genius, who would protect the kitchen

The Porto Praenestina (now the Porta Maggiore) in Rome with the Aqua Claudia and the Anio Novus running on top of it. To the right is the tomb of the baker Marcus Vergilius Eurysaces and his wife Atistia

The Arch of Titus was erected in AD 81–82 by Domitian to commemorate Titus's and Vespasian's conquest of Jerusalem. Reliefs display the booty carried from the Temple of Jerusalem including the Menorah (seven-branched candlestick), and the triumphal procession. The arch was in such a bad state in the nineteenth century that it was dismantled and reassembled, integrating several missing pieces

Trajan's Column, 38m (125ft) high, erected in AD 113, consisting of 29 drums of marble. Once crowned with a statue of Trajan, it now has a statue of St Peter. The frieze tells in 155 scenes the story of Trajan's two campaigns over the Dacians. Originally it stood in a courtyard with a library at either side and a basilica at one end

Hadrian's mausoleum for himself and his family on the banks of the Tiber was finished in AD 139. It was incorporated into the city fortifications from the third century AD and was converted into a fortified castle from the thirteenth century. It is now the Castel S. Angelo

A view of the Senate House from the Forum Romanum

Above: View of Pompeii from the Tower of Mercurio

Left: A shop at Herculaneum showing charred shutters

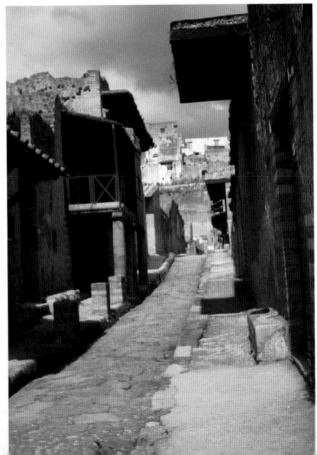

Above right: House at Herculaneum showing the method of building by *opus craticum*

Right: A street in Herculaneum with a two-storeyed house on the left

Part of the funerary relief of a man and a woman. (Museo Nazionale Romano, Rome)

Tombs in the necropolis outside the Porto de Nocera, Pompeii.

Model of a necropolis. (Rheinisches
Landesmuseum, Bonn)

The tombstone, dated c.AD 160–170, of Gaius
Julius Maternus, veteran of Legion VI Minervia
displays an example of a funerary banquet scene.
He reclines on his couch with a beaker of wine
in one hand and a napkin in the other. Before
him is a table, probably displaying fruit. His wife
sits to one side in a basket chair and a servant
ready to pour more wine waits on the other side.
(Römisch-Germanisches Museum, Cologne)

An elaborately carved sarcophagus with an elephant. (Musei Capitolini, Rome)

The Temple of Apollo, Pompeii. The statue of Apollo, represented as an archer, is a copy of the original found on the site

The House of the Vestal Virgins, Forum Romanum, Rome. This was rebuilt around a peristyle garden about AD 113. The statues, now arranged on the north side of the court, were found in a pile at the west end and are believed to be Head Virgins dating from the third and fourth centuries AD

Bust of Commodus with the headdress of a lion skin identifying himself with Hercules. (Musei Capitolini, Rome)

Above: The Lararium in the House of the Vettii, Pompeii

Left: Bronze statue of Aesculapius. A serpent, symbol of healing, winds itself round the staff.
(Musei Capitolini, Rome)

The Great Bath at Bath, England, was part of the complex surrounding the healing shrine of the goddess Sulis-Minerva

A mosaic representing theatre masks. One, with flowing locks, is tragic; the other is comic representing a satyr. They lie on a plinth in front of a wall against which rest two flutes. (Musei Capitolini, Rome)

A view of the Hippodrome, Istanbul (Constantinople), where chariot races were staged. The obelisk, which was in the centre of the spina, was brought from the Temple of Amon in Karnak and set up in AD 309. It rests on a base showing the Imperial family watching chariot races

Amphorae of various shapes found in the Villa Regina, Boscoreale, Italy

The Via Stabiana, Pompeii, was a north–south road leading between the Porta Vesuvio and the Porta di Stabia. To the left is one of the many public fountains. On the top of the pillar on the left was a small tank from which water could be distributed through pipes let into the pillar. Wheel ruts in the street are clearly visible

Funerary monument from Neumagen, Germany, early third century AD. It depicts a warship of the German fleet with 22 oars and a steering oar carrying barrels of wine. (Rheinisches Landesmuseum, Trier)

House of the Stags, Herculaneum. The pergola would have overlooked the sea. The marble table stands in its original position

Above: Carving of a deer set on by hounds in the House of the Stags

Right: Statue of Augustus in the role of Pontifex Maximus with his toga drawn over his head. (Museo Nazionale Romano, Rome)

The Forum Romanum looking west with the Arch of Septimius Severus and the Senate House. Looming behind is the enormous monument to Victor Emmanuel II built to honour the Unification of Italy in 1870

SHOPS

Town houses were not necessarily just living areas. The distinction between home and workplace was not clear-cut in the Roman period. Jashemski's excavations suggest many gardens were exploited for profit, growing vegetables, having orchards or even vineyards of over 100 vines. Householders did not allow their gardens to be completely ornamental. They might be cultivated to provide recreational areas but they had to pay their way. Excavations at Pompeii have revealed agricultural tools in houses indicating an intention of cultivating produce for sale.

Many of the larger houses had a place of business incorporated into their frontage. The House of Sallust at Pompeii had a bar (*thermopolium*) at the front of the house. Shops, run by the householder or leased to tenants or clients, could be fitted out with paintings and mosaics to indicate their wares. Small establishments could have two rooms on the ground floor; the front room was the shop and the rear room the living quarters. There would be a counter at the front and wooden shutters closed the building at night. Charred remains of some shutters have been found at Herculaneum. Counters were wooden tables or permanently fixed ones; many had marble frontages. Some counters were built round huge jars, which could have held *liquamen*, olive oil or wine. Horizontal or upright racks could hold amphorae. Some establishments at Pompeii and Herculaneum have been recognised as bakeries. They had huge bread ovens and small mills turned by donkeys or slaves.

Living quarters in these shops would be simple. Mats were used as beds, which could be rolled up during the day. In some Pompeian houses there is a shallow indentation in the wall of

Shop at Herculaneum showing dolia incorporated into the counter

a room. These are presumed to be 'bed niches' where a person could lie out of the way of the rest of the household.

During the later empire, lines of shops were constructed with a colonnade in front to provide a pleasant retail experience. In other parts of the empire shops have been identified by strip houses. A workshop or shop would be the room open to the street. Behind would be the living quarters and at the rear a stable or industrial yard. Doorways at the side of the premises led into a narrow alley. Tile-built hearths provided cooking facilities. These types of shops have been identified in London but they were probably common in other parts of the empire as they are economical in space.

VARIATION IN HOUSE DESIGN

Houses style was not static. Status mattered but housing had to reflect appropriate status. The house should not be more opulent that the occupant deserved, otherwise it could be regarded as pretentious and possibly dangerous if it excited envy. Petronius mocked the freedman

Fresco now in the Museo Archeologico Nazionale, Naples and originally from the House of the Century. It depicts Vesuvius with Bacchus on the left holding a thyrsus. Below is the serpent Agathodemone (the great god) indicating fertility

Trimalchio for having opulent living conditions. There would be a continual programme of building and rebuilding, hence the wide variety of houses to be found in Pompeii and elsewhere. Some houses in Ostia, Pompeii and Herculaneum had rooms which had been converted to industrial processes; several had rooms converted to fulleries. Not every householder wished to preserve his house as his ancestors had done. Pompeian houses reveal the wide variation of atriums built; the style was sometimes dependent on where the house was situated on the street, sometimes on the taste of the householder or the builder he employed. The House of Octavius Quarto has a set of rooms round the atrium, and two others set round smaller courtyards. Behind one is a long garden with a water channel. The House of the Golden Cupids has all its rooms set to one side with on the other a very large peristyle.

Some houses were small with one or two rooms on a ground floor, about 3m (10ft) square and a loft reached by a wooden ladder. There would also be a small kitchen and a latrine area. Some were built in the back garden of a large house indicating a shortage of building plots or individuals selling off private land. Many streets in Herculaneum had small and large houses in the same street. Some houses were constructed of wooden square frames filled with stones and mortar (*opus craticum*). Interior partitions were of flimsy lath and plaster. Both were economical fast building methods. Many houses were of two storeys, the ground floor devoted to a shop or a business and living quarters on the upper floor reached by a wooden ladder. The rooms were small often placed round an inner courtyard. One family, who had a shop on the ground floor and an upper floor with red plastered walls, fled when Vesuvius erupted leaving their possessions: two beds, a wooden cabinet, a cupboard for utensils, a wooden shrine with a bust of wood probably representing an ancestor, statues of the household gods and a gaming set. Graffiti on one wall read, 'Basileus still resides at Puteoli'. Perhaps the family did get away safely and took shelter with this man.

VILLAS

Another form of housing was the villa. There were several types. The villa *rustica* was in the country, the villa *urbana* was just outside the town and the villa *maritima* was situated by the sea built near a town or in the country. Some could be large complexes such as those of Pliny the Younger who owned several villas, described in a letter to Gallus, one at Laurentum, 17 miles from Rome, which he visited in the winter and spring, and another described in a letter to Apollinaris in the Tuscan Hills near the source of the Tiber which he visited in the summer and autumn. He often came to collect rents from his tenant farmers and to settle disputes. Some Romans had more than Pliny. Cicero had eight large villas, his favourite being one at Tusculum, besides smaller ones on the coast.

The Villa of the Papyri near Pompeii was excavated in the eighteenth century and its owner must have enjoyed a luxurious lifestyle. Its length was approximately 1000 Roman feet, 244m (800ft), situated above a beach with private docks and boathouses with stairs leading to the villa level. The atrium opened into a square peristyle with columns on each side and a large pool in the middle. This led into an antechamber with beyond it a long peristyle 101m (330ft) long, 37m (122ft) wide, lined with 64 columns. In the centre was a large fishpond 38.7m (127ft) long and 4m (13ft) wide. Beyond this, at the end of a gravelled pathway was a belvedere.

An aqueduct and an ingenious hydraulic system supplied water to fountains and pools. The villa contained 90 pieces of sculpture, 13 large, 18 medium and several small bronzes, 32 bronze busts and 15 marbles busts. The most exciting discovery was a library of 1787 rolls of papyrus, which the owner of the villa had lovingly collected. Unfortunately most of these were destroyed when attempts were made to open them. The few that have been opened revealed the owner's cultural tastes.

On the other hand a villa might be a small working farm, run for profit, such as those described by Columella, Cato and Varro, whose owners might live in them or have a house in the town and place a bailiff in the villa to care for it and ensure the crops were well tended. The villa was also seen as a place for the owner to relax. Horace praised his little farm in the Sabine Hills, which his patron Maecenas had given him. A villa provided status in society, and could be highly profitable, allowing for expansion, and many were in the third and fourth centuries AD with magnificent dining rooms and other apartments. Cato gave much advice on how to make a villa profitable, emphasising the need for excellent storage, including a well-built barn and plenty of vats for oil and wine. The owner would then benefit from good prices, and 'it will redound to his wealth, his self-respect and his reputation'. Under no circumstances should the property decline in value for this might affect the displays of *liberalitas*, which were an essential part of public life. The surplus of the estate produced wealth for owners to provide gifts to the community in the form of public feasts and buildings.

Some officials and military men who bought villas introduced new plants, which they had brought back with them from their campaigns. The expansion of the empire also introduced new fruits, vegetables and herbs. Better breeding methods were established in the provinces, thus benefiting local agriculture. But the villa owners were concerned only with their own properties. There was no wish to buy run-down properties in order to improve them. The most sought after properties were prosperous ones, which provided a good income. What mattered was social standing as compared to the estates of other owners. Acquisition of land, no matter how poor, was valued more than improvement to increase the value of all estates.

As the Romans extended their empire many people saw the merit of living in comfortable conditions while running a profitable farm. In Britain and Gaul this form of living was taken up enthusiastically, especially those who had embraced classical education and Romanised concepts. By the fourth century AD some villas in those areas were amongst the largest known in the Roman world. These were based on the courtyard style, having numerous rooms and a large bath suite, which provided a social function for visitors invited to dine. In Britain their development can be traced from long-range buildings such as that at Park Street to the splendid complexes of North Leigh, Woodchester and Chedworth.

HOUSEHOLDS

In the household there was an intertwining of function and relationships. Domestic tasks were performed by the women and slaves, economic and political decisions were taken by father and sons. The household was male dominated and the father had supreme power, even that of condemning his children to death. An example is that of Lucius Brutus. Valerius Maximus said that when Lucius found that his sons were trying to restore the tyranny of Tarquin whom he

had expelled, he arrested his sons and ordered their execution. Thus he put aside his role as a father and assumed that of a consul devoted to the Roman state.

The term 'family' went beyond an immediate family of two generations. It included those who were dependent on the head of the household – slaves and their children, freedmen and foster children. The father was the *paterfamilias* who held paternal power with the right of taking all decisions. His children had no right to own or maintain property or to marry or divorce without his consent. He could compel his children to divorce a spouse. He could not sell his daughters into slavery but he could sell his sons. He had also the right to expose his newborn children, a method of limitation of the family in the ancient world, except if they were healthy sons.

Sons therefore only became legally independent on the father's death. If the father had not made a will all the sons and unmarried daughters shared equally in the estate. If a son had died his children received the father's share divided equally between them. It was assumed that the family was an economic unit working together and the members of the household had the good of that household at heart. Survival in childbirth was not guaranteed and the continual deaths of children could result in the survival of only one son. Many men adopted a son so that the practice of a single person inheriting was common. He would then have to be responsible for other family members.

In the empire some of these paternal rights became restricted. By the third century AD a father who killed his child could be prosecuted and the Emperor Hadrian exiled a man who had killed his son because the latter had been having an affair with his stepmother. Even so, the father's right to expose the newborn child still continued in spite of the attempts of the Emperors Constantine and Valentinian to prevent it.

On marriage all the rights that a father had over a daughter passed to her husband. Roman writers liked to indicate the absolute authority of the husband. Valerius Maximus told the story of Egnatius Maecenius who killed his wife for being drunk. No one considered prosecuting him because 'all right-thinking men considered that she deserved what she got because of her lack of self-control. It is agreed that any woman who drank without restraint puts any virtue she may have at risk and risks fully paying for this vice.'

As women were not counted as Roman citizens they could not vote or hold political office. What power they had was exercised by sheer personality as is obvious from the careers and actions of women in the imperial household. Livia, Augustus's second wife, gained considerable influence in public life. She advised Augustus on political matters and was industrious in charitable activities. Augustus granted her and her sister Octavia, who had married Mark Anthony, a special grant of sacrosanctity that allowed them to be financially independent and to be protected for their own actions which assumes that he expected them to act independently. Livia sponsored buildings, festivals and religious offerings. After her death she was deified as her husband had been. Statues of her show her carrying a cornucopia identifying her with the goddess Fortuna. In the third century Elagabalus granted more public honours to his mother, even allowing her a seat in the Senate. For the first and only time a Senate of women was set up on the Quirinal Hill which devised a complicated code of etiquette for women including 'what clothing might be worn in public, who was to yield precedence and to whom, who was to advance to kiss another, who might ride in a chariot, on a horse, a pack-animal or on an ass, who might ride in a litter' and details of wearing jewellery.

As a mother a woman was responsible for raising her children. She was responsible for the education of girls but how far they were educated was at the father's discretion. Girls could become highly educated, but they were just as likely to only learn to sew and weave, behave discreetly and modestly and manage certain parts of the household. The epitome of a good wife was summed up on a tombstone at Rome erected in the first century to Amymone, wife of Marcus, which said 'She was good at working wool, pious, modest, frugal, chaste and content to stay at home.'

Boys' education was possibly only for those in the higher ranks of society. Poorer children had to help on the farm, in the workshop and at other trades as soon as possible to relieve the burden on the family. Quintillian said that education must begin early, arguing that a child should develop according to his age. Plutarch said that families often chose Greek tutors and that there were a great many of these. Some Romans, such as Cato, preferred to educate their own sons at home as he did not think that his son Marcus 'should be indebted to a slave for such an eminent thing as education'. He therefore wrote his own history of Rome to acquaint the boy with ancient traditions and heroes. He also trained the boy in boxing, wrestling and swimming and paid particular attention to his moral education, avoiding saying any indecent word in the child's presence. The boy, however, had such a feeble constitution that Cato had to relax what was a severe regime.

If not educated at home, boys went to school, but it depended on the character of the schoolmaster as to whether the boys learned anything. Plutarch said that when a seven-year-old boy hit the head of his teacher with his writing tablet, the father praised the boy saying that he was a spirited lad. Tacitus said that teachers might resort to toadying to their pupils but given their lowly status, for many were slaves, they would have hardly dared to defy the father who paid them. Cicero took the teacher's part saying that it was parents who were at fault for refusing to allow their sons to profit by stern discipline.

Given all the problems it was surprising that any boys were educated but it was essential that they could read and write in both Latin and Greek and had knowledge of Roman traditions if they were to follow a career path. Suetonius said Augustus trained his foster sons in administration and business while they were still young; his daughters he merely trained in spinning and weaving. There was always a network of relatives and friends to act as advisors so that boys could learn skills in oratory and be prepared for military service. Education seems to have been more by transmittance of ideas and example than by formal classes. Horace paid tribute to his father who saw that he was taught studies that any senator would have taught his own offspring.

The woman's main task was to run a household smoothly. Columella gave instructions on the duty of the wife of a farm bailiff. In rainy weather and at times when she could not do any agricultural work she should occupy herself with sewing and weaving. She must go round the household daily seeing what tasks needed to be done. She should supervise the slaves, who were equally part of the household. In some households there might be a freedman in charge of the slaves but the wife was expected to give him orders to ensure the household's smooth running. When she went out she would be accompanied by a slave and often travelled in a litter to avoid the dirt and bustle of the streets. Many women would have some if not much latitude in what they did. They were not confined to the home and in a household run by slaves would have had a considerable amount of leisure time.

CLIENTS

Clients were part of the household in the sense that they could be dependent on the patron's generosity and be linked to him in return for services rendered. The relationship was a binding moral contract. Dionysius said that for both patrons and clients it was unlawful to accuse each other in lawsuits or bear witness. Anyone who did so could be guilty of treason. Patronage required suitable receiving rooms, for clients had to be kept separate from family members, although if the master of the household was absent his wife stood in. Clients were expected to attend in the morning in order to seek help and advice. They might even be invited to a meal to discuss business or, with an unscrupulous patron, to become involved in plots to advance his candidature or particular cause. They were expected to vote for their patron, speak well of him and be available to carry out his wishes. The higher the status of the patron the better for the client and to have gained the ear of a consul or even the emperor meant that advancement was assured.

Bust of Lucius Caecilius Jucundus found in Pompeii. Wax tablets found in his house provided information of his business activities including auctions of a variety of objects such as slaves and furniture

DRESS AND APPEARANCE

Dignity was essential to a Roman household and outward appearance mattered. How a man dressed indicated his station in life. Magistrates, senators and any man with pretensions wore a toga varying from beige to brown in colour. Victorious generals wore a purple toga, a colour later assumed by the emperors. The toga was a difficult garment to wear, being a huge semi-circular piece of material 5.6m (18.5ft long) and 2.13m (7ft) across at its widest point. Magistrates and senators had a broad purple stripe along the straight edge; equestrians had a narrow stripe; mourners wore one of black or a dark colour. Candidates seeking office indicated their intention by wearing one of bleached white; otherwise it was made of unbleached natural wool.

The arrangement of this garment was complicated for it was placed over the left shoulder, taken round the back, brought under the right arm, and back over the left shoulder, any folds being gathered over the left arm. The left arm was always covered, the right left free. It was pulled over the head when making a sacrifice or on an official occasion. Skill was required to make the drapery fall easily and as the weight was considerable men had to walk slowly, which prevented any rash movement, particularly where weapons were concerned. Slaves often followed their masters to rearrange a toga if it slipped. Suetonius said that Augustus ordered the *aediles* to see that it was worn by everyone in the Forum and that he always kept a toga in his bedroom in case he had to be called out hastily. Martial envied Linus living in the country, who wore his toga only twice in a month.

Most men wore a tunic, belted at the waist and reaching to or below the knees. Over this or the toga was thrown a hooded cloak (*paenula*) or a loose fitting cloak (*lacerna*). Juvenal referred to his *lacerna* as his '*toga protecta*' and Martial recommended its use covering the toga on a chilly day in the amphitheatre. This garment was usually black but it was customary to wear a white one in the amphitheatre. Martial mocks Horatius who wore a black one that in a sudden snowstorm turned white. In wet weather Martial recommended a leather cloak (*paenula scortea*).

Bronze statue of a man dressed in a toga

Two men wearing togas, possibly from a funerary monument

Beneath the tunic men might wear a loincloth. Roman men did not wear trousers as these were consider the mark of a barbarian, but as the empire extended and men found themselves in colder regions this prejudice broke down. The army wore breeches and by the end of the empire breeches and trousers were a common form of dress.

Men were clean shaven and had short hair during the republic and in the early empire. In the later first century they had a short clipped beard. Numerous barbers were available to attend clients either in the street or at the public baths. Martial mocked a visit to the barber; 'Part of your jaws are clipped, part is shaved, part plucked of hairs. Who would imagine this to be a single head.' He advised them to avoid the barber Antiochus if they wished to avoid scars on the chin. Pliny the Elder recommended spiders' webs soaked in oil and vinegar to staunch this bleeding. Nevertheless a visit was essential if a man wished to hear the latest gossip. It was probably with some relief that during Hadrian's reign fashion began to follow the emperor's dense, curly beard. Even then beards and hair were oiled, especially at banquets.

The usual dress for Roman women was a loose, long tunic (*stola*) over which was draped a shawl (*palla*) and they could wear a scarf (*focale*) at the neck. They might have a *mappa* over the arm to wipe the dust from the face. Under the *stola* they wore another shorter tunic and controlled their breasts by a soft leather strap (*stophium*). When out walking they were protected from the sun by a parasol, which as it could not be closed, would be carried by a slave.

During the republic hair was drawn back over the head and gathered into a bun, with occasionally a fringe of curls at the front. Juvenal mocked the contrast between the height of a woman seen from the rear and in front; 'You would not think she was the same person.' Women regularly ordered their slave to pluck grey hairs from their head. Some women wore blond wigs made from the hair of captured German women. Hairstyles became more elaborate in the early empire, with hair held in place by pins or combs, resulting in a mass of curls at the front and the rest of the hair braided into a bun, so that many households had a personal hairdresser or competent slave to achieve an elaborate result. Juvenal lamented an unhappy slave girl who fails to arrange a coiffure correctly and might have her own hair torn out, her tunic ripped off her and be whipped at the behest of an irate, screaming woman.

Women also needed cosmetics. Creams and perfumes were commonly kept in glass phials or alabaster jars. White chalk was painted on the cheeks and brow. Ochre tinted lips, soot or powdered antimony coloured eyebrows. Ovid recommended a facemask of eggs, vetch, skimmed barley, pounded narcissus bulbs and honey. Spots, he said, should be covered with patches or powder. Powdered horn could enamel teeth. Martial satirised Galla even if she offered him 'an infinity of delights': 'You lay aside your teeth at night ... and your face does not sleep with you.'

Men and women wore sandals, light ones indoors, heavier ones for the street. A closed boot had to be worn with the toga. Men, especially those in the army, wore a heavy hobnailed boot made from layers of leather with a closed upper. Sometimes these had wooden soles. In the provinces many people wore socks and leggings. Jewellery was prolific. Women wore necklaces, rings and earrings; men wore rings, which also acted as seals. Both wore brooches to fasten their cloaks. These were often placed in graves so that they could continue to enhance themselves in the afterlife.

Statue of a woman
wearing a *palla*

5

FRINGES OF SOCIETY

PRAETORIAN GUARD

I t might be strange to include soldiers on the fringe of society, but Rome was at first wary of military power. It was not until the second century that legions were stationed in Italy. Until then the emperors needed a bodyguard of armed men. This was the duty of the Praetorian Guard, originally a small group of men who accompanied republican praetors on a campaign and guarded their headquarters. Augustus retained his former guard of nine cohorts, each 500-strong, rotating them so that there were not more than three in the city of Rome at any one time. Tiberius housed them in barracks, the Castra Praetoria on the edge of the city beyond the Servian Wall. By then the guard numbered 12 cohorts. Vitellius added another four but Domitian reduced them to 10.

Two equestrian prefects, answerable directly to the emperor, commanded the Guard and a tribune and a centurion commanded each cohort. Praetorians were paid three times the legionaries' salaries and could resign after 16 years. They wore togas except when on military duties so as not to alarm senators who were unaccustomed to seeing soldiers in Italy. Dio Cassius said that the Praetorian Guard was trained as a legionary force and wore the same uniform. Their distinguishing mark was a thick plume springing from a long box on their helmets. Their standards were so heavy that Caligula permitted them to load them onto the backs of mules when they marched.

If they wished they could become legionary centurions; it was hoped that their loyalty to the emperor would be spread to the wider army. On discharge they would receive a bronze diploma giving their legal status as a veteran and detailing their career. Vespasian granted them the right to immunity from taxation for land given to them by him and for any property they had owned before he granted them this privilege. Legionaries could transfer as did Gaius Maccenius Vibius whose tombstone in Rome records that he served nine years in Legion X Gemina before transferring to the Guard where he served for another 14 years.

The guard was paid by the emperor but in addition received a larger donation than that given to the ordinary legionary. Augustus left 250 denarii for each praetorian as opposed to 75

denarii for the ordinary legionary. Claudius, realising only too well his debt to the Praetorian Guard who had helped to create him emperor as he quivered behind a curtain, gave each man 3750 denarii and both Marcus Aurelius and Lucius Verus increased this to 5000. They also received substantial donations at festivals and were always open to bribes. Nero granted them a free allowance of grain each month.

Their main duty was to ensure the safety of the emperor and their formidable reputation gave them the sense not only that they were an elite body of troops but also that they were able to enforce their will regardless of public opinion. In AD 98 they forced Nerva to punish the men who had killed Domitian who had favoured them. Early coins of Claudius make clear his debt to them. The praetorians are shown greeting Claudius and the text reads 'Praetorianus Receptus'. They had an excellent opinion of themselves. The tombstone of Quintus Caetronius Passer, who served in the guard for eight years, noted 'I lived as I wished properly, in poverty and honourably. I cheated no one and may that assist my shade.'

The historian Edward Gibbon was scathing, commenting on 'the praetorian bands, whose licentious fury was the first symptom of the decline of the empire.' He said that 'Augustus, that crafty tyrant', had 'formed this powerful body of guards, in constant readiness to protect his person, to awe the Senate, and either to prevent or to crush the first motions of rebellion.' They were indeed powerful and this resulted in a disgraceful episode in the late second century. In December AD 192 Aemilius Laetus, Prefect of the Guard, conspired with Marcia, Commodus's concubine, to kill the emperor. The Guard then made Pertinax emperor, as he assured them he would give each man 12,000 sesterces. Pertinax, however, not only refused to pay this, but also tried to stop the Guard seizing plunder for themselves. They therefore elected Sosius Falco, one of the consuls to be emperor, when Pertinax was in Ostia dealing with the food supply. Pertinax returned, exiled Falco, but neglected to take precautions for his own safety and was killed. The Guard then auctioned off the city and empire. Didius Julius won the empire by offering each soldier 250,000 sesterces. This was to no avail. He did not get the support of the Guard, who murdered him.

News eventually reached Septimius Severus who was pronounced emperor by his soldiers at Carnuntum in Pannonia. Herodian said that when Septimius arrived in Rome he ordered the Praetorian Guard to parade leaving their weapons behind, as was customary when they escorted emperors to a festival. They came expecting to swear an oath of allegiance and to receive the usual donation. Instead soldiers surrounded them. Severus said that 'he had netted them like fishes in a circle of weapons' and men superior in intelligence had captured them. He dismissed them, ordered them to go beyond the hundredth milestone from Rome and appointed a completely new guard, with increased pay, recruited from the Danubian provinces. He also placed a newly formed legion, the II Parthica a few miles south of Rome. Dio Cassius said that when was he was dying, Septimius advised his sons: 'Do not disagree. Give money to the soldiers and despise everyone else.'

The guard continued until AD 312 when they backed Maxentius for the empire and were included in his defeat at the Battle of the Milvian Bridge. Constantine dissolved them, destroyed their camp and their cemeteries and replaced them with a largely German mounted guard, the Scholae Palatinae (named after a portico in the palace where they awaited orders) that had been founded by Diocletian in AD 284.

Bust of Constantine

VIGILES

Augustus established seven cohorts of *vigiles*, 1000-strong, headed by an equestrian prefect, which acted as a fire brigade. They were equipped with lanterns, siphons, buckets and axes. Each unit was assigned to two of the 14 districts into which Rome was divided. Augustus had intended them to be temporary but they were so useful that they remained a permanent force. They were first recruited from freedmen and Tiberius granted citizenship to those who completed six years of military service; later Roman citizens were recruited. Claudius stationed a cohort at Puteoli and another at Ostia. Both they and the urban cohorts could be called on to defend the emperor in a crisis. At first they lived in lodgings or at home until Nero provided

Courtyard and shrine of the House of the Vigiles, Ostia

barracks for them and their equipment. In AD 205 Septimius doubled their numbers but they remained cramped in the old barracks. By the fourth century they had lost their military role and were civilians employed by the city.

OTHER SOLDIERS

The Praetorian Guard was supported by a group of horsemen but the early emperors employed a troop of Batavian and German horsemen who served until a revolt in Batavia resulted in a lack of imperial confidence. They were disbanded and in AD 98 Trajan recruited a new unit (*equitates singulares Augusti*), 1000-strong, which was stationed on a camp of the Caelian Hill. When Septimius Severus arrived in Rome he dismissed them and founded a new mounted guard, double in size and stationed in two camps under two tribunes. These served emperors both as a guard when they were away from Rome and as a control and ceremonial unit in Rome. In AD 306, however, the Roman troops joined Maxentius in his bid for the empire and were defeated at the Battle of the Milvian Bridge. Constantine destroyed their camp replacing it with the Lateran Basilica and depicted their demise on a panel on his triumphal arch.

Three urban cohorts were stationed in Rome to act as a police force. Other forces guarded the imperial mint at Lugdunum (Lyons) and the grain warehouses at Ostia. In the second century more cohorts were recruited who at first were answerable to the city prefect but then came under the control of the Praetorian Prefect. These numbered 500 but by the time of Septimius Severus had been raised to 1500.

Left: Bust of Septimius Severus

Below: The Emperor Caracalla

Other troops seem to have included 300 scouts (*speculatores*) and a *numerus* of *Statores Augusti* used as military police. A group of *Peregrini* acted as military, or even secret, police, carrying out the emperors' personal orders. Another group of about 100, the *Frumentarii*, established by Trajan, acted as couriers and possibly spies. In addition there were sailors from the Ravenna and Misenum fleets stationed on the Esquiline near the Colosseum who were employed in working the awnings on the amphitheatre, but were also used as couriers. In Galba's reign Tacitus mentioned troops from Illyria being encamped near the Campus Martius. Later Caracalla brought German and Scythian troops to Rome. It is clear that there must have been a considerable presence of troops in the capital that would have made the citizens aware of the emperor's power.

SLAVES

Slaves were traded like any other commodity and slave traders, though despised, were accepted as a necessary evil. Strabo noted that one of the trading commodities of pre-Roman Britain was slaves. He also referred to the slave market on the island of Delos, which could sell or buy 10,000 slaves a day from east or west. The result, he said, was that merchants said a proverb was coined, 'Unload your ship, everything has been sold'.

Slaves would be carefully inspected to see that they were in good health. Sales were carefully regulated. The dealers must be honest about a slave's accomplishments and faults. Aulus Gellius said that *aediles* ordered that placards placed round the neck of slaves should be legible, indicate any fault and state if he or she were runaway slaves, thus implying they were less trustworthy. Pliny the Younger, in a letter to Plinius Paternus wrote, seemingly with some doubt, 'I think the slaves you advise me to buy look all right but it remains to be seen if they are honest'. He would have preferred a more personal recommendation for he added that you could not go by looks of slaves but rather what you have heard of them.

It is difficult to estimate the value of the cost of a slave. Dwarves and Ethiopians cost more than older men and women. Martial said that he bought a slave he believed was an idiot for 20,000 sesterces, but then demanded his money back. Pliny the Elder said that Marcus Scaurus paid 700,000 for Daphnis, a skilled linguist, while Clutorius Priscus paid 50 million sesterces for Paezon, one of Sejanus's eunuchs. Such a sum, if accurate, either displays his worth as a slave or is an example of the conspicuous consumption which characterised Rome.

Roman society relied heavily on slave labour, indeed it was believed that the economy and social life could not function without slaves. Slaves had few or no rights; Cato in his description of their work on farms viewed them quite dispassionately, detailing their workload, their number for the size of the estate and the controls which should be placed over them. Most slaves had been captured in one of the many wars fought by Rome, especially those against the Gauls and Carthage. Caesar, when he defeated the Gaulish tribe of the Veneti after their revolt in 56 BC, determined to make an example of their defeat. He executed the leading citizens and sold the rest of the tribe into slavery. The defeat of Carthage is estimated to have resulted in 60,000 people being taken into slavery. Josephus reported that during the Jewish War the total number of prisoners taken was 97,000. Males over 17 were sent to work in Egypt or to fight in the arena.

Pirates often attacked merchant ships, stealing the cargo and selling crew and passengers as slaves. In the fourth century AD a pirate raid on the coast of Britain captured the future St Patrick who was sold into slavery. Much earlier in 76 BC pirates captured the youthful Julius Caesar as he was sailing to Rhodes. For once they had met their match. As soon as he was ransomed, he gathered together some ships, captured the pirates and ordered them to be crucified. They could not complain about their punishment; Caesar had stated what he would do on his release. Because they had treated him well he did give them the privilege of having their throat cut to save them the agony of crucifixion. He could quite easily have sold them as slaves.

Plutarch said that the tax burden levied by Sulla on people in Asia in 85–84 BC was so heavy that people sold first their sons, then their daughters and then themselves. Others did the same. Peasants who were unable to till or sell their land found slavery attractive. Unwanted or abandoned children were taken into slavery. Some estates bred slaves believing that slaves bred to slaves became slaves. It would be impossible for a slave owner to keep all of these.

Some would be left to die. The owner could have reared them and sold them at a profit but many preferred not to have that expense.

Criminals who had committed serious crimes were sent to work in the mines, quarries, engaged in other hard labour or sent to fight in the arena. Emperors used slavery as a punishment and Suetonius said that they would sell informers into slavery.

Slavery continued throughout the empire, even after the introduction of Christianity, which theoretically offered equality for all. St Paul's *Epistle to the Galatians* stated: 'There is neither Jew nor Greek, male or female, there is neither bond nor free: for ye are all one in Christ Jesus.' But his *Epistle to the Colossians* noted: 'Servants be obedient to your master in all things.' St Peter was equally adamant: 'Servants be submissive to your masters with all fear; not only to the good and gentle but also to the harsh.' Substitute slave for servant and the effect was to enforce the legitimacy of slavery. The emphasis was to be on hope of an eternal life, not alleviation of one's lot in this one.

Christianity made no attempt to abolish slavery. Monasteries and bishops' sees therefore employed slaves. Justinian's laws codified the trade and treatment of slaves, but slavery was never abolished. Gradually, however, fewer slaves were kept. Masters found it difficult to feed and supervise such large numbers of people, who were resentful of their status. It required, however, a complete change of moral consciousness for the total abolition of slavery and that was not to happen during the Roman Empire.

Public Slaves

Public slaves owned by the state or towns worked in temples, bathhouses, civic buildings and assisted officials such as aediles. The hardest work was in the mines or the quarries. Strabo said that 'the air in the Spanish mine at Mount Sandaracurgium, was deadly because of the smell of the ore'. The workforce needed to be over 200 but the miners became so exhausted by disease that they had to be continually replaced. Slaves might have the opportunity to be trained as gladiators. They would be provided with decent food and if they fought well could gain their freedom.

Imperial slaves (*servi Caesaris*) served the emperors in their numerous palaces. Each one would have his own task. Frontinus in speaking of the water supply mentioned that Marcus Agrippa had his own gang, which he bequeathed to Augustus, and Augustus in his turn willed them to the state.

Private Slaves

Many estates could not have been run without slaves. Cato, Varro and Columella all give details about how slaves should be treated and the work expected of them. Tacitus said that Pedanius Secundus, a Prefect of the City, had 400 slaves in his household, but was murdered by one of them, either because he refused to manumit him (set him free) or because he was his catamite and wished to be the catamite of another man. Seneca gave an example of one of the worst masters: Vedius Pollio ordered any slave who annoyed him to be thrown into a pool of vicious fish. Large estates left the supervision of slaves to a bailiff; on smaller farms the owner had to keep

an eye on his slaves. Either way they were treated as farm stock. Cato said bluntly each year 'check your livestock and hold a sale'. Amongst the things for sale would be slaves.

Slaves in city households might have had an easier time. Well-educated slaves, often Greeks, became secretaries, tutors, accountants and doctors. A tutor or a nurse could build up a rapport with a family. Those who worked in shops or industries could have a harder time, but slaves in towns had the great advantage that they could be paid wages. In theory they could not own anything as the money belonged to their master, but some masters allowed slaves to save the money to buy their freedom. Pliny the Younger even allowed his slaves to make wills which were legally binding. They could then distribute their possessions within the household. Slaves could marry if their masters allowed this, but they were still his property. Women and young boys were particularly vulnerable to sexual advances made by a master.

There was always tension in the life of a slave as to whether he would be punished for a minor transgression, whether to conceal his real thoughts, whether to risk a contemptuous gesture which would bring punishment, even whether he might be alive at the end of the day. To protect themselves many slaves joined guilds which provided company, festive dinners and, above all, ensured that they would have an honourable burial.

Slave Quarters

It is often difficult to know where slaves were housed. Slave quarters were probably placed near kitchens and latrines. One has been identified at Rome in the remains of an apartment block. Thirty small rooms at the bottom of one at the foot of the Palatine Hill near the Arch of Titus could have held about 50 slaves. Nearby another had a corridor from which five undecorated rooms led off on each side. These are also suggested to have housed slaves. The House of Menander at Pompeii had four small undecorated rooms in a row next to a kitchen and latrine which have been identified as slave quarters, probably monitored by a freedman and giving easy access to the house. A similar set of rooms was identified in the House of the Century with a side entrance to a nearby street. Slaves could also be housed in cellars or in the upper floor of a house. They might have slept where they could. Slave nurses slept with the children. Apuleius in *The Golden Ass* said a slave slept outside Milo's bedroom door. Pliny the Younger said that slaves in his Laurentian villa slept in rooms which could also be used by freedmen and guests. The master of the household had a dilemma in wishing his slaves both to be seen and not seen. They reflected his political, social and economic status but they should carry out their duties discreetly and without disturbing his routine. The leg irons found in the House of Venus reveal that they were made to understand their status. In the Villa of the Mosaic Columns situated outside the Porta Ercolana a skeleton was found with similar chains clamped to his legs; this slave had been forgotten as his master fled from the eruption.

Freedom

There was a way out of slavery. Slaves could buy their freedom or be manumitted. They might earn it for good reasons – if they had served their master well, or as Dionysius of Halicarnassus

stated because 'they had assisted their masters in a crime, even murder, and this would prevent them from being called to give evidence against him.' Some masters freed slaves in their wills so that they could praise his good deed. Slaves, when freed, could become clients of their master, thus giving him great prestige. Slaves might be freed if they became too old to work and therefore a burden on the household. They then became a burden on the state. Suetonius said that Augustus would not permit the manumission of more than a limited number of slaves and ruled than no slave who had been tortured or kept in prison could become a Roman citizen.

Masters could make slaves free by informal methods such as inviting them to dinner. Usually freedom was given at a legal ceremony before a magistrate. The master would touch the salve with a rod and declare that he or she was no longer his property. He then slapped the slave indicating the moment of freedom. Freedom granted in wills was carefully worded otherwise the heir might claim back the slave.

FREEDMEN

Once a slave was freed, various careers opened up. They could become imperial freedmen acting as secretaries and carrying out public missions as Narcissus did for Claudius. So influential was he that Agrippina had him killed after she had murdered Claudius. Greeks were especially valuable and in the early empire they formed a useful civil service. Many freedmen had successful careers. A poem by Statius gives the story of Claudius Etruscus who worked in Tiberius's palace as a slave, was manumitted and 'raised to the highest office.' He seems to have been away from Nero's court but under Vespasian he was put in charge of the treasury, of finances for decorating imperial palaces and of production in the imperial mint. So well did he do that Vespasian raised him to the equestrian class. Although Domitian exiled him, he returned to Rome and died in AD 92 aged 90.

Tombstones record others having retail or professional careers – architects, surveyors, doctors and oculists. Many became bailiffs, overseers or stewards or were loyal servants of serving military officers. Only freedmen could become one of the *seviri Augustales* who organised emperor worship and *vicomagistri* who organised the worship of Stata Mater, the goddess who protected Rome against fire.

PROSTITUTES

Brothels existed throughout the empire and prostitution was not considered a criminal or a moral offence. Lower class inns and taverns and public baths also offered this service to their customers, as did independent prostitutes working from their own house or hired room. Brothels attached to baths usually opened in the afternoon so that women who bathed in the morning would not be disturbed. Many of the women were slaves or foreigners, as Horace and Ovid said, often from Syria or Egypt and girls were sold at auction for this purpose. Hadrian, however, forbad anyone to sell a slave to a procurer without giving a reason. Martial mentioned that Gellianus, an auctioneer getting desperate to sell a girl and wishing to prove she was clean, 'drew the unwilling girl to him' and kissed her four times. It availed him nothing. 'A bidder of six hundred sesterces withdrew his bid.'

During the republic prostitutes were able to marry Roman citizens but this was forbidden under the empire, which also restricted their right to inheritance and legacies. Prostitution was regarded as a profession and it was not considered immoral for prostitutes to accept money for services rendered. They had to register with the aediles and Caligula made them pay a standard fee for a single act of intimacy although it is doubtful how this could be continually policed.

Prostitutes were recognised because they were wore heavy makeup and were garbed in a brightly coloured short tunic rather than the long *stola* of a Roman matron. If they plied their trade in Rome on the street they were usually found, according to Martial, on the Via Sacra or in the Subura. Juvenal said they were at the Circus Maximus along with fortune tellers, palmists and phrenologists. There were numerous brothels in Rome. In one of his Satires he portrayed Messalina, the emperor Claudius' third wife, disguising herself as she made for a brothel which had her own reserved room, where she took 'all comers, For cash, without a break' and was always the last to leave. Several brothels were identified at Pompeii. On the ground floor of a two-storied one, owned by African and Victor, were a number of cubicles for clients leading off a central hallway where presumably the clients waited. Each room had a stone bed on which would be placed a mattress. Obscene paintings and graffiti make it quite clear what was the purpose of these rooms. Juvenal described Messalina's cell as having stale bedclothes and being lamp-smoked, stinking and filthy which indicated the disgusting conditions in which some prostitutes worked.

Given this complete acceptance of intimacy with prostitutes there must have been cases of syphilis and gonorrhoea, but there are few references in the writings of the time. One allusion is in a letter which Pliny the Younger wrote to Calpurnius Macer saying that when he was sailing on Lake Como a friend had pointed out the house where a woman had roped herself to her husband and together they had thrown themselves into the lake because 'he was suffering with ulcers in his private parts.'

COURTESANS

Courtesans were in a different category from prostitutes. They were groomed for their role, were often cultured, good conversationalists, well read in the classics, competent dancers and entertainers and attentive to a man's needs. They had excellent table and party manners and were trained to hold their drink well. A procuress might secure the courtesan a lover. He was expected to provide an elegant living establishment with servants in attendance. A courtesan, however, had no security. She could be ejected from the house at a moment's notice especially if the man felt that she was unfaithful. Like prostitutes, under Augustus' law she was forbidden to marry and ran the risk that when she lost her charms she might face an impoverished old age or be forced into prostitution.

Most courtesans were freedwomen, who, like prostitutes, had to be registered with the aediles. Some married women took up the profession, but Suetonius said that Tiberius was furious about this. He exiled some and Tacitus said that the Senate refused to allow women to be registered whose husband, father and grandfather were or had been senators or equestrians. Whether this did stop women being courtesans is uncertain as the profession had a certain glamour and allowed women some freedom. It may have been that some husbands connived

at this, assuming that their wives would gain some reward either pecuniary or a chance for patronage. Horace, however, was horrified at the exploits of one young woman who consorted with travellers and Spanish sea captains. Ovid detailed all the instructions needed and gave advice to help her to keep her lover satisfied. He also explained how she might engage in other assignations while keeping her main lover, even to the extent of sedating him while she exerted her charms elsewhere.

CONCUBINES

Women living with men without being married to them were *concubinae*, who were expected to have all the virtues of a wife but not her privileges. They were usually women of a different status from the man, such as a freedwoman, especially as Augustus had decreed that senators were not allowed to marry freedwomen. A widowed man with children might prefer a concubine to another marriage, but any children were not considered legitimate. If the concubine was a slave the man had an obligation to free her and to give her rights to some property. Soldiers often kept concubines before they were able to legally marry in AD 197 and men kept them if the family was unable to provide a dowry.

Women did not get the same freedom. Claudius forbad free women to cohabit with slaves and his imperial freedman Pallas drafted a law, which was passed by the Senate in AD 52, stating that if a free woman married a slave without the consent of his master she would be reduced to the status of a slave; if he gave his approval she would be reduced to the rank of a freedwoman. If children resulted, they were slaves. If women freed male slaves in order to marry them they ran the risk of public disapproval and Septimius Severus issued a decree against such marriages.

Emperors had concubines. Suetonius said Vespasian accepted Antonia Caenis, his former mistress, as his concubine after his wife's death. Marcus Aurelius took the daughter of his steward after the death of his wife, Faustina. He did this to avoid marriage with Fabia to whom he had been betrothed in his youth and to have a companion for his children. Concubines often had great powers of patronage and were treated with respect. Suetonius criticised Domitian for being discourteous to his father's former mistress. However, Commodus' concubine, Marcia, was part of the conspiracy that killed him.

Later emperors did not limit themselves to one concubine. Gordian II indulged himself with 22 concubines from all of whom he had three or four children, thus being nicknamed Priapus after the Roman god of fertility. Constantius was probably the son of Claudius II by a concubine and his son Constantine was the son of his concubine, Helena. Constantine also had a concubine by whom he had a son Crispus.

6

STAGES OF LIFE: BIRTH, MARRIAGE, DEATH

BIRTH

The Romans practised contraception to limit families. Aristotle suggested that cedar oil, white lead or frankincense, should be applied in the ulna. Hippocrates mentioned drinking *misy*, diluted copper sulphate. Pliny the Elder suggested cedar oil rubbed over the penis as a male contraceptive. Oribasius preferred inserting a pessary of cabbage into the uterus after intercourse. The only obvious remedy was *coitus interruptus*, which Lucretius said prostitutes used but this was also suggested by a Greek physician Soranus, who practised in Rome in the second century AD. He also provided sensible advice saying that intercourse should be avoided at periods suitable to conception, that is, after menstruation. He also recommended pessaries of wool soaked in honey, olive oil and cedar resin alone or with white lead. Olive oil does reduce the mobility of the sperm, thus diminishing the possibility of conceiving. More bizarre methods included using the heart of a lion killed in the arena. Women coped with menstruation with a tampa of lamb's wool or a nappy that could be washed.

The alternative to contraception was abortion and Roman writers spoke of a range of methods. Soranus mentioned poultices, baths in various substances and insertions into the vagina. There seems to have been no law against abortion – Suetonius said Domitian forced his niece Julia to have an abortion – until Septimius Severus decreed that a wife should be punished if she aborted without her husband's consent. Infanticide and infant exposure were also allowed, especially if the parents could not afford to bring up a child or if the child was deformed. A boy was more welcome than a girl but too many sons diluted an inheritance, so they were still at risk. To stop this practice, emperors would often give money to poor parents. Children of slaves were regularly exposed or killed. Excavators of the Hambledon villa in Britain revealed at least 97 infant burials indicative of this practice.

Miscarriages were frequent. Pliny the Younger wrote to the grandfather and aunt of his third wife that his wife had miscarried because she had neglected to take reasonable precautions and did things which should have been avoided; 'Indeed,' he wrote, 'she could have died.' To give birth

women often sat on a chair with an opening in the seat or on a stool. A funerary relief from Ostia depicts a woman sitting on a chair. Behind her an assistant or slave grips her shoulders. The midwife sits on a stool while she extracts the child from the mother. Soranus said that a midwife should have a soft skin, long fingers and short nails. A surgeon might use his instruments to ease the birth but many women gave birth in fields or homes and were expected to work almost at once. Both mothers and their children frequently died during childbirth, from infection, haemorrhaging and puerperal fever. Frequent pregnancies were also responsible; women might have to bear five children to ensure that one survived. Cornelia, the mother of Tiberius and Gaius Gracchus, had 12 children; only three survived. Excavations at the Roman cemetery of Poundbury in Dorset have revealed that 51 out of 281 females died probably during or after giving birth.

Tombstones depict these losses. At York, Felicius Simplex mourned Simplicia Florentina 'a most innocent soul' who lived nine months. At Mainz, Telesphoris and her husband mourned for their 'very sweet daughter', aged 20 months, 'Oh that you had never been born, when you were so loved.' Death was no respecter of social class. Fronto wrote a bitter letter to Marcus Aurelius lamenting the loss of five children: 'grief upon bitter grief is multiplied.' Marcus Aurelius had 10 children; only one son, Commodus, survived, and Commodus's only son died in infancy. Cicero, however, said that many people in Rome thought that if a small child died the loss must be borne calmly; if a baby it must not be lamented. Funeral rituals were expensive and so 'this burial would be a hasty affair.'

On the whole the birth of a child, especially a male child, was welcomed as it continued the dynasty. Birth could be a public occasion. There was no feeling of privacy. Relatives wanted to witness the birth if only to assure themselves of the status of the child. The child's father was admitted after the birth so that he could decide whether the child was to be reared. If it was, he raised it up high. An offering was made to Juno Lucina, goddess of childbirth. Other public ceremonies might take place to ensure the survival of the child. On the eighth or ninth day the child was named and in accordance with a decree of Augustus the child had to be registered with the state.

Bust of Marcus Aurelius

Bust of Cicero

Wet nurses reared most children of the upper classes, many being slaves, freed women or Greeks being taken into the household for that purpose. Soranus said that they should be sympathetic and self-controlled. Childhood was not regarded as a separate stage in life but a boy did have a ritual introduction into his birthright, usually when he was 15. He then donned the *toga virilis*, probably on 17 March, the festival of the Liberalis. The family would go to a temple to make a sacrifice, and then return to the house to make another to the household gods. From then on a boy would be expected to follow the *cursus honorum* where possible. Pliny the Younger wrote to Minicius Fundanus that if anyone asked what he had done in a day one of the events would be a coming-of-age, ceremony, a betrothal or a wedding; he implied that there were a good many of these.

MARRIAGE

A father had to consent to the marriage of either a son or a daughter. The mother might be involved and no doubt was subtly active behind the scenes but she had no legal right to dispute her husband's choice. Both the state and the family regarded marriage as an institution for producing legitimate children. Illegitimate children could be adopted and become Roman citizens but legitimacy was preferred as a means of determining status and passing on property from one generation to the next. When a census was taken the question was put 'Have you married for the purpose of creating children?' Aulus Gellius reported that Spurius Carvilius Ruga in 235 BC was the first Roman since the founding of the republic to divorce his wife on the grounds that she was barren and that he did this because he had taken an oath before the censors when he had married that he had done this for the purpose of having children.

In Plautus play *Aulularia* Eunomia tells her brother she has a plan for his welfare, 'I want you to marry so that you may procreate children, may the gods grant it!' Suetonius reported that Julius Caesar had numerous affairs and mistresses and that a Tribune of the Plebs had stated

that following instructions he had drawn up a bill to be passed during one of Caesar's absences from Rome legitimising Caesar's marriage with any woman 'for the procreation of children'. Suetonius mentions a comment by the Elder Cato that Caesar was 'every woman's husband and every man's wife.'

Marriages were also used to form alliances, especially with the political elite. Men would marry because they saw the advantage in gaining a family network to assist them in securing a career and to give them support when needed. Pliny the Younger wrote to Junius Mauricus – who had asked him to search for a husband – that Minicius Acilianus would make a splendid husband for his niece because Minicius had reached the office of praetor with great distinction thus sparing the necessity of canvassing on his behalf. Cicero, when in exile, was supported by his brother-in-law Atticus in Rome and his son-in-law Calpurnius Piso Frugi. A network of supporters was always useful.

Marriage between the children of friends was always welcome. Cicero's brother Quintus married Pomponia, the sister of Cicero's great friend Atticus. Pliny's letter to Junius expresses his delight that he can do his friend a favour by suggesting marriage. Young romantic love played no part, or if it did, had to be assured of parental agreement. If the woman in question was a widow, however, she might be able to express an opinion.

Plutarch said that the Elder Cato married his young wife when he was an old man. He asked one of his under secretaries, Salonius, had he found a good husband for his daughter? Salonius said that he had not and would not do so without consulting Cato. Cato then replied he had a suitable husband for her and when he revealed it was himself Salonius was amazed, not only because he thought Cato too old but because she was far beneath an alliance with a consul. When he realised Cato was in earnest he gladly agreed.

Pliny the Younger was in his forties when in AD 100 he married his third wife Calpurnia who was in her teens. She was all he wished. He wrote to her aunt Calpurnia Hispulla, 'She is highly intelligent and careful with money and her devotion to me is a sure indication of her virtue.' When he pleaded in court she arranged for slaves to report to her on his progress. She had an interest in literature, kept copies of his writings to read again and again and memorised them. She listened to his poems and even set some to music, chanting them to a lyre. To Pliny who loved an audience this must have been very gratifying.

The proposed bride could be betrothed but was not of marriageable age until she was 12. Once a marriage had been agreed a betrothal party could take place at which agreements (*sponsalia*) and gifts took place. In some cases these were part of a dowry, which was considered to be part of a payment towards running the expense of an increased household. It could be a grant of land and or cash in instalments and had to be commensurate with the father's status. Roman law allowed 10 months for these payments to be completed. Pliny wrote to his friend Quintilianus that he knew Quintilianus was not blessed with so much wealth as he was of intellect. He then made a generous offer. 'I am taking upon myself as part of your responsibility and in the capacity of an additional father to settle on our girl, 50,000 sesterces.' This would enable her to keep up the style of being married to Nonius Celer.

Cicero's daughter Tullia was 12 when she was engaged and 16 when she was married in 67 BC. He husband died 10 years later and she then remarried, but the marriage was dissolved in 51 BC. Cicero quickly agreed to another marriage but was forestalled by Tullia and her mother who had agreed her marriage to another suitor. Octavian (later Augustus) betrothed

his daughter Julia when she was aged two to the son of Mark Anthony. Later, however, because he found many men were betrothing themselves to infants to avoid marriage he decreed that the betrothal would not be valid unless the man married within two years. He stated that men should be married before they were in their twenties. Marriage of close relations was forbidden, but by the first century marriage of first cousins was allowed. Freeborn Romans could not marry slaves although this seems to have been ignored in the provinces.

Once betrothal had taken place the parties concerned were considered to be one family, which meant they could not be compelled to give evidence against one another. Either party, however, could sue the other for breach of promise. The engaged couple became *sponsus* and *sponsa* and the union was sealed by a kiss and the placing of an iron ring on the third finger of the woman's left hand. That finger was chosen, according to Aulus Gellius, because it had some communication directly to the heart.

Roman law stated that if two persons lived together it could be considered a union but marriage entailed a ceremony and a celebration. The right day had to be chosen and the auguries consulted. Certain dates were impossible – the Parentalia when the spirits of the dead walked the earth, the dates of the opening of *Mundus*. Each month had unlucky days such as those commemorating national disasters and, of course, the Kalends, Nones and Ides. The other days of the month were possible but the best dates were those in June.

In the early days of the republic the marriage ceremony was one of bride-purchase. The man paid a nominal sum to the father for the right of having his daughter. Later in the empire the marriage could be a lavish celebration. For the woman, or in many cases a girl, it was her entrance into society. During the republic she had to weave a special tunic, which was worn the night before the wedding. She could weave a veil for the ceremony, which was taken off when the couple stood face to face. Some of this continued into the empire. She was expected to put away her childhood toys the night before the wedding.

The procession of the groom to the bride's house was as elaborate as the groom's circumstances allowed. Marriage ceremonies for wealthy families, and especially those who held high office, might be conducted by the Pontifex Maximus and priests and include expensive sacrifices, together with the eating of ritual foods – salt, cakes and fruit. For other households it was a simple ceremony where the ritual words were spoken, '*Ubi tu Gaius, ego Gaia*' ('where you are male, I am female' or 'to whatever your family, I now belong.') Sacrifices were made to Vesta and to the household gods, and a figurine of the Genius was brought to the groom. The marriage contract was signed and witnessed by some of the guests. The wedding feast that followed would be as lavish as could be afforded. Juvenal mocks 'the blushing bride hung round her husband's neck at a lavish wedding breakfast ... Why waste money on a reception to well-gorged guests.' Better to concentrate on the 'first-night bridal offering.'

After the feast the bride was escorted to her new home accompanied by many ribald comments. Torchbearers led the way and small boys danced around them. A pinecone symbolised Ceres, the goddess of the earth. Once the bride reached the house she placed wool on a doorpost and smeared it with fat to indicate wealth and well-being. The groom presented the bride with a goblet of water. She was carried over the threshold lest she might trip, touched fire and water (the basic elements of a household) and then paid homage to her new home's household gods.

DIVORCE AND ADULTERY

It would be impossible to say how many marriages were successful. The fact that divorce was permitted indicates that some failed, but marriage confirmed status and produced legitimate children, making it socially attractive. Some were also clearly very happy. Cicero relied on his wife's support during his exile. He ends one letter urging her to take good care of herself: 'My Terentia, most faithful and best of wives, and my most beloved little daughter and remaining hope.' Ovid, when also in exile in Tomis on the Black Sea, wrote poems addressing his third wife in fond terms, 'dearest', 'my light', 'greatest wife'. 'You hold more than half my heart.' Pliny the Younger tells the story of Arria who begged to join her husband Paetus in exile. She was refused but hired a small boat and sailed after his ship. She also shared his wish to commit suicide by dashing her head against a wall. Many tombstones also indicate the loss of a loved husband or wife.

Men did have mistresses and women had lovers. Roman poetry, especially that of Catullus and Propertius, imply that love affairs were constant. A dinner party could be a dangerous time. Ovid suggested that a lover attracts his beloved's attention with discreet nods, glances and playing footsie. Lucullus threw Cato's half-sister Servilia out of her home for her sexual indiscretions and Cato divorced his first wife Atilia for similar behaviour. Augustus's laws on marriage and adultery in 18 and 9 BC made his attitude clear. If a wife was adulterous the husband should immediately divorce her and he had the right to kill her lover. Both might be exiled. The adulterer could not remarry a free born Roman citizen. Augustus was concerned with raising the crime of abusing a man's honour into the crime of abusing the institution of marriage. A dual sexual standard occurred, as men were not punished so severely as women. A wife could not prosecute her husband for adultery as in law he had committed no offence, even with a married woman. She could, however, get her father to prosecute him through a law intended to presume chastity of women on marriage. Augustus forced his favourite Polus to commit suicide when he was discovered to have been seducing married women.

DEATH

The Romans were more concerned with how a person died than the cause of death. An ideal death was to meet it bravely. Some deaths were ignominious – assassinations, forced suicides and murders. Ammianus Marcellinus said the Emperor Valentinian died (AD 375) speechless, sweating, breathless, grinding his teeth, flailing his limbs and covered in an agonising rash. To many, death might be relief. Juvenal cringed at

> old men looking alike, their voice and body trembling, head quite smooth, a baby's dripping nose. The pathetic creature has to munch his bread with weaponless gums ... the delights of food and wine are no longer the same as his palate grows numb and as for sex, it is now a distant memory.

Far better as Plautus in *The Two Bacchises* said, echoing Menander, 'He whom the gods love dies young while he has his strength, senses and mind.'

Dying was a public event and therefore the right ceremonies had to be performed. When a person died the closest relative gave the last kiss to catch the soul, closed the eyes and began a formal lament with arms outstretched, including the *conclamatio*, when the name of the deceased was cried aloud. A man would be dressed in a toga, a woman in a long robe. A coin was placed in the mouth or on an eye to pay Charon a ferry fee across the River Styx. A wealthy family might have a lying in state as that depicted on the relief of the Haterii family. Flaming torches were placed at the head and end of the bed. A seated woman at the foot of the bed played a mournful tune on a double pipe.

Senators and important persons might have their corpse placed on the Rostra in the Forum, and a colleague or friend would give a eulogy emphasising both the merits of the deceased and those of his ancestors. A wax or wooden portrait of the deceased joined other ancestral portraits in the house. Pliny the Elder said that before his time wax masks were stored in cupboards and brought out for family festivals. These were not death masks but representations of the dead. Suetonius remarked that when Vespasian died his favourite comedian Favor was chosen to wear his funeral mask in the procession and give the customary imitations of his gestures and words, which suggests that funerals were not always solemn occasions.

BURIAL

The law of the Twelve Tables, observed until the late empire, did not permit burial within the walls of any Roman town or city so that the bodies did not pollute the earthly world physically or spiritually. A boundary stone at Rome set up by the praetor, Lucius Sentius, declared that by decree of the Senate for the public good no corpses were to be buried beyond that marker near to the city. Nor should there be any dumping of rubbish. It adds menacingly 'Take shit further out if you want to escape trouble.' An exception to burial within the city was made in the case of emperors. The Twelve Tables also decreed that funeral expenses were to be minimal but Cicero said that few people bothered to observe this.

The first burials in Rome were inhumations but possibly because of the lack of space both inhumation and cremation was practiced from the eight to sixth centuries BC. Pliny the Elder said that cremation was instituted after it was discovered that bodies were being dug up for some unknown purpose. Lucretius said that the Romans embalmed their dead but this implies that bodies were then buried rather than cremated. Tacitus recorded that Nero was passionately fond of his wife but in a burst of anger he kicked her to death. He then had her embalmed 'after the fashion of foreign courts' by stuffing the body with spices before arranging her burial in the Mausoleum of Augustus. Cremation, however, seems to have been the normal practice during the late first century BC and into the first century of the empire. Inhumation began again in the second century and then became universal throughout the empire during the third century.

Servius in a commentary on Virgil's *Aeneid* said that cremation took place at a specific place, an *ustrine* or *ustrinum* within a cemetery. If a person was cremated on a pyre placed at the exact place of internment the site was called a *bustrum*. Goods were placed on the pyre – jewellery, clothing, food, even small animals so that these would accompany the deceased to the otherworld. Pliny the Younger wrote to Attius Clemens that when Regulus's son died his father had all his ponies, dogs, parrots, blackbirds and nightingales slaughtered and placed on the pyre. 'This was not grief, but parade of grief.' Everything had to be completely consumed.

Then the pyre was doused with wine and all the ashes collected. The wealthy placed them in caskets; the poor in a pit. There was still social distinction in death, but the poor contrived to have the deceased buried in a cemetery with a pipe leading into the grave into which libations could be poured.

What was important was the survival of the soul after death, a belief that the Etruscans had held. The Epicureans and Stoics believed that the soul dispersed at death or lost its individuality but many Romans believed that there was life after death. Treatment of the body depended yet again on status and wealth. Poorer people might be thrown into open ditches outside a city along with dead animals and rubbish. Suetonius said Nero was nearly thrown from his horse when it smelt a dead body lying alongside a road. Slaves and workmen paid money to *collegia* so that the correct burial rites would be performed. The *collegia* might have *columbaria* where ashes could be placed thus giving dignity in death.

Columbaria contained numerous semicircular or rectangular niches to hold the ashes of the dead. Some were discovered outside the Aurelian Wall near to the Via Appia. Others have been found much closer to Rome but still outside the city. In some of the niches urns (*ollae*) containing ashes have been discovered still in their original resting place. One *columbarium* outside the Servian Wall was a three-storied structure, built partly underground, with an upper room for funereal banquets and two lower stories provided with niches. An inscription records that this was constructed for Tiberius Claudius Vitalis either for his family or to rent out for his clients.

Columbarium at Ostia

Funeral processions for wealthy people were usually held at night, organised by undertakers (*libitinarii*) and a master of ceremonies, with musicians followed by the grieving mourners. If the body was to be cremated a finger would be cut off and buried to commemorate the former burial practice. Poorer people held burials during the day and had to make do with relatives carrying the body. Tombs of the wealthy can still be seen outside Rome lining the Appian Way and the routes from Pompeii. The dead might be placed in lead lined coffins or elaborately carved stone ones. Gypsum could be poured over the body forming a cast.

After the burial, services had to be rendered. The relatives returned to the house for the rites of purification by fire and water. The house had to be cleansed. Funeral feasts were eaten at the grave on the day of the funeral, another on the ninth day, after which a libation was poured to the Manes (the spirits of the dead). On anniversaries relations and friends ate commemorative meals at the tomb, and a share was always put out for the deceased. The fact that it was not eaten did not mean that the dead spirit was not partaking of its share; it would be nourished either within its bones or its ashes. To help in the preparation of such meals, kitchens were sometimes provided at mausolea. Such kitchens can be seen attached to some tombs at the Isola Sacra cemetery at Ostia. These tombs present the appearance of the dwellings of a well-to-do bourgeoisie. The premise of the tomb as an eternal home was a constant in the Roman world. Trimalchio decorated his tomb carefully: 'It is wrong to look after the house in which you live and to neglect the house in which you will stay much longer.'

Meals could be eaten in the funerary gardens, created round a tomb. Trimalchio, when giving directions for his future tomb, said that he would like to have an orchard with 'every kind of fruit growing round my ashes and plenty of vines'. The Romans had a passion for gardens. The Elysium Fields, to which many hoped to go, were regarded as an idyllic landscape with abundant flowers and heavenly banquets. The alternative was Hades, described by Ovid as a dark, gloomy place ruled over by Dis where wandered lifeless shades without flesh and blood.

Lid of a sarcophagus; the style of the lid suggests an Etruscan origin. (Museo Nazionale Romano Rome)

Funerary relief of a shoemaker,
(Musée Saint-Rémi, Reims)

These practices were widespread throughout the empire. In the catacombs of Kom el-Shuqqafa at Alexandria, Egypt, dating from the second century AD, the dead were interred in a vast necropolis, reached by a spiral staircase, descending to a depth of 35m (115ft). A triclinium with three stone benches was provided, where meals could be eaten before the dead underwent the ritual of evisceration and mummification, so graphically represented on the wall of the principal tomb. Anubis, the Egyptian god of the dead, but here dressed as a Roman legionary with a serpent's tail, representative of the Greek divinity, Agathodaemon, and Sobek, the crocodile god, also depicted in Roman military dress, guarded the embalmed body, before it was incarcerated within one of the many niches carved out of the rock. When the catacombs were first excavated, wine amphora and tableware were found on a central wooden table in the triclinium.

The dead were recorded on tombstones, found throughout the empire. The tombstone of Marcus Valerius Artemis, freedman of an architect at Pompeii, recorded a sentiment which became commonplace, 'Traveller, passer-by, what you are, I was; what I am now you will be.' But Titus Cissonius at Pisidian, Antioch, a veteran of Legion V Gallica, exhorted 'While I lived I

Sarcophagus found at Simpleveld. (Reproduced by permission of the Rijksmuseum van Oudheden, Leiden, The Netherlands)

drank freely; you who live drink.' Bodies could be placed in elaborately carved sarcophagi. Some show statues of heroes and deities; others have figures of Bacchus. The labours of Hercules were popular as these denoted the trials a hero could face. Other coffins, for the less well-off were of wood or terracotta.

From the first to the third centuries AD there was a fashion for representing figures placed on funerary couches, which may have been copied from the Etruscans. Sometimes the figures are recumbent; sometimes they are sitting up. A somewhat similar scene, which derived from the Rhineland, is reproduced on reliefs in the northern parts of the empire. These display the deceased sitting on a couch, sometimes with a wife or slaves, holding up a beaker, indicating a funerary banquet. Other reliefs, especially in Gaul, portray trades and occupations of the diseased. Obviously these people did not wish to be forgotten after death. One of the most remarkable examples of this is to be found on a coffin found at Simpelveld in Holland. Seemingly a wealthy lady had been placed in a stone sarcophagus. On one side of the coffin was carved her effigy lying on a couch. Carved round the sides were all the amenities she could wish for in the Otherworld – furniture, jars which possibly contained wine and oil, cupboards which hid her household and personal possessions, and even, for maximum comfort, a bath-house. In the furthermost reaches of the empire this lady had embraced the Roman way of living and a Roman vision of life after death.

7

STATE AND PERSONAL RELIGION

RELIGIOUS BELIEF

Roman religion was not a monotheistic faith but a series of practical actions mainly concerned with rituals to appease the gods. It was hoped they would provide assistance and refrain from generating disasters. The Romans were fearful of invoking divine wrath and certain rituals were performed to avoid this. Valerius Maximus said that the Romans worshipped gods to make them beneficent to men while Cicero said he failed to see why the gods should be worshipped if men neither received nor hoped to receive benefits from them. Roman religion, therefore, was a series of bargains made between men and deities.

Roman religion entailed private and public ceremonies; it provided shrines and temples where the gods could be worshipped, together with a staff of officials to supervise ritual and provide instruction in worship to a divine hierarchy; it ensured a code of conduct and practice. Above all it was extremely tolerant of other religious cults, welcoming their worshippers and their practices. Only in two areas was there hostility: druidism because of the practice of human sacrifice, and Christianity because of its opposition to plurality of gods in favour of a monotheistic one.

Temple of Apollo, Pompeii. This has an imposing flight of steps leading to a high podium, which once had six columns supporting a pediment. In the distance is Vesuvius

SUPERSTITION

There was an element of superstition in Roman religion. Warnings might be given in a dream or natural phenomena, flight of birds, the death or sickness of an animal, lightning, unexpected storms, fire, epidemics and earthquakes. Roman writers mention darkness at noon, shooting stars, swarms of bees, showers of blood, oil and milk, doors that opened and closed themselves. Anything that could not be explained could be a portent. It was then necessary to let the gods know that the message had been received and to placate them by some action.

The Twelve Tables issued a warning against bewitching anyone or casting evil spells. Pliny the Elder related a case of a freedman being envied by his neighbours because he produced such good crops, saying he had gained these by spells. He was summoned before the magistrates, but appeared with well-made tools and well-fed oxen to show that it was hard work and care of livestock which produced results. He was unanimously acquitted. Pliny also gave suggestions for actions which should be taken to avert the evil eye. A canine tooth taken from an unburied corpse could be an amulet, but there were many other devices. Amulets, part of Roman jewellery, would accompany their owners to the grave to ward off evil. Phalluses, a crescent moon and the swastika were popular.

Women, in particular, were accused of practising witchcraft. Horace in one of his satires spoke of witches digging up bones from the cemetery on the Esquiline Hill, where criminals and paupers were buried. Elsewhere in his *Epodes* he describes Veia digging a hole with an iron mattock to bury a boy up to his neck. When he died his liver was cut out and used as a love charm. Curse tablets (*defixiones*) are frequently found, even in distant parts of the empire. These sought vengeance on the perpetrators of a theft or an insult following a certain formula because, like all such invocations, the form of words was vital. Their sonorous rhythm suggests the hand of a professional scribe. One found in the baths at Bath demands the return of a silver ring crying that not only the person who has stolen it but anyone who knows anything about it or keeps silence will be cursed in (his/her) blood, eyes and every limb and have all intestines eaten away.

Livy recorded Appius Claudius Crassus in 368 BC speaking about religious scruples, 'What difference they will say if the sacred chickens do not feed; if they are slow coming out of the coop; if a bird utters an ill-omened cry. These are trivial things but it is because the Roman fathers did not neglect them that they were able to build a great republic.' Cicero warned that it was a citizen's duty to weed out superstition and that credence should be observed when listening to a soothsayer: 'As signs may be perceived in anything, no one who believes all of them can ever remain in a tranquil state of mind.' A man could choose not to see anything. Cicero gave the example of Marcus Claudius Marcellus, consul five times and a successful general in the war against Hannibal. When he wanted to avoid superstitious belief, he travelled in a closed litter so that he would not see anything to disturb him. Suetonius said that superstition never deterred Julius Caesar. When he fell as he disembarked on the coast of Africa, he immediately turned the situation to his advantage by clasping the ground and saying 'Africa I have you in my grasp.'

THE ROMAN CALENDAR

The practice of religion was controlled by a calendar of festivals and games. The details have been deduced from literary sources and fragments of surviving reliefs fixed to walls in Rome and other towns in Italy, most of which were set up during the early empire. These dates, enhanced over the centuries, incorporated ancient practices and beliefs. Macrobius said that Numa began the calendar dividing the year into months and the months into days, calling each one a working day, a festival or a half festival. At first the calendar had a 10-month year; later it was extended to 12 months.

A year normally had 355 days. March, May, July and October had 31; February had 28 and the other months 29 each. Constant adjustments kept this calendar in line with the solar years so periodically 22 or 23 days were added. This led to difficulties, especially when the calendar was deliberately altered for political reasons. Eventually Julius Caesar reformed the calendar in 46 BC. The Julian Calendar, with some adjustments has remained in use to the present time.

The Romans reckoned the days of their months by three fixed dates. The Kalends was the first day; the others were the Nones and the Ides. In March, May, July and October the Nones were on the seventh day and the Ides on the fifteenth. In the other months the Nones were on the fifth and the Ides on the thirteenth. All the other days were reckoned by being counted before the Kalends, the Nones and the Ides. Some religious ceremonies were held on fixed days, which were linked to the phases of the moon. The Kalends were sacred to Juno; a sacrifice of a pig or a lamb was offered on the sighting of the new moon. The priest would then announce on which date the Nones and the Ides fell. On the Nones, when the moon had reached its first quarter, the dates of the holidays were announced. The Ides was sacred to Jupiter as were the dates of the full moon and a sacrifice of a sheep would be offered to the god. Dates of festivals and other days were announced. Markets, for example, were held on every eighth day. Towards the end of the republic the number of days in the week was reduced to seven.

The days were divided into hours, 24 to each day, but each hour could be longer or shorter according to the time of the year. Daylight and night time hours varied although midnight was always the sixth hour of the night and noon the sixth hour of the day. An hour during the summer months could be about 90 minutes; in winter it could be 45 minutes. This was because the longer hours of daylight allowed a longer working time.

Some days, regarded as unlucky, had to be avoided. These were days when some unlucky event had taken place such as the Roman defeat by the Gauls in 390 BC and the three days (24 August, 5 October, 8 November) when the *Mundus* was opened, regarded as the Gate of Hades when the spirits of the dead might return to haunt the living. These were, according to the Roman poet Festus, days when only things that were absolutely necessary were done. People must avoid beginning things: no one should marry, start a voyage or a lawsuit.

In addition certain dates were considered to be favoured or ill omened; pious Romans might have to consult a calendar or rely on memory to see what they could or could not do on certain days. Petronius says Trimalchio had an inscription above the doorposts in his dining room headed, 'presented to C. Pomponius Trimalchio, Priest of the College of Augustus by his steward Cinnamus.' A wooden tablet on one post said 'our Gaius is dining out on 30 and 31 December'. The other displayed representations of the phases of the moon and the seven heavenly planets. Different coloured studs marked lucky and unlucky days. The average person would certainly have wanted to know market days, what was the best date to get married or start a law suit. At first only the priests knew the details of the calendar, which gave them considerable power, but from 304 BC calendars were placed in the forums of important towns.

PRIESTHOOD

Roman religion had two forms, that controlled by the state and that practised by individuals. The state religion needed trained men to perform religious rites and ceremonies and to regulate the *ius divinum*, the law controlling the relationship between the divine and the human. During the monarchy the king was the state-priest and *paterfamilias* of his people. During the republic the chief priest, the Pontifex Maximus, was assisted by a *Rex Sacrorum* who controlled sacrifices and sacred matters. Gradually his role was subsumed into that of the Pontifex Maximus. In the empire the emperor became the Pontifex Maximus and the *paterfamilias* of the State, thus reverting to the role held by the kings.

The Pontifex Maximus, who had a house at the Regia in the Forum, was assisted by two colleges of priests, the pontiffs and the augurs. These were magistrates, who accepted a priestly role as part of their career structure. The pontiffs controlled the calendar and organised religious festivals. Dionysius of Halicarnassus said that they had to ensure that rituals were performed without error to explain and interpret these rituals to the general populace. Although laymen, they had to be skilled in religious knowledge. Religion and politics therefore intermingled and one could manipulate the other.

By the end of the republic the College of Pontiffs numbered 16 who held office for life. They were in charge of festivals, sometimes having to pay for them out of their own resources. The college included *flamines*, priests attached to the cults of certain deities. The three major ones were linked to Jupiter (*flamen Dialis*), Mars (*flamen Martialis*) and Quirinus (*flamen Quirinalis*). 12 other *flamines* were attached to certain festivals. They wore an *apex*, a conical or round cap on which was placed an olive stick surmounted by a strand of wool and a *laena*, a thick woollen cloak. These were symbolic of the two most useful gifts to men.

The *flamen Dialis* was restricted by many duties and taboos. Aulus Gellius gives a list that includes riding a horse, taking an oath, wearing a ring with a stone in it, having no knots in his clothing, and not allowing a slave to cut his hair. Hair and nail cuttings had to be buried under a fruitful tree. He could not lead an army so a consul could not be the *flamen Dialis* or vice versa. As the consulship was an essential part of the career structure it is not surprising that given this and the irksome taboos, the office had lapsed by the end of the republic. The title was later assumed by the emperors to emphasise their religious function.

The College of Augurs numbered 16 men who oversaw the layout of temples and interpreted signs to decide whether the gods approved or disapproved of certain actions. Whatever augurs decreed to be ill-omened or unlawful was to be declared null and void. They had to be consulted before any state action was undertaken and did this by consulting the auguries. Livy indicated that the duty of consulting before a war dated back to the late seventh century BC when Attius Navius, a famous augur, insisted that no innovation could be introduced until birds had given their approval. The then king, Tarquin the Elder, who was fighting the Sabines, wanted to raise more cavalry and was furious at this check to his plans. He mocked Attius saying. 'Inquire of

these augurs what I am now thinking will come to pass.' Attius said that he had taken the auguries and what the king thought would surely come to pass. The king said, 'Get to perform what your birds say is possible.' Whereupon Attius cut a stone in two with a razor. From then on, Livy concluded, auguries and the augur priesthood were held in great respect. Nothing was done without the auguries being taken, including meetings of popular assembles, mustering of the army and acts of great importance.

Cicero said that augurs did not foretell the future. This was the role of soothsayers and haruspices, who had originally come from Etruria. Haruspices foretold the future by standing with one foot on the earth, the other on a stone, and examining the organs of sacrificial victims, especially the livers and entrails. These indicated the name of the divinity to be approached. A diseased liver could indicate disaster. Models of livers were marked with names of deities. One found at Piacenza in north Italy had the divisions of the heavens marked which linked the haruspices with astrological lore. They were not priests and by the end of the republic their influence appears to have waned. The emperor Claudius revived their practices and established a college for them in AD 47.

Cicero derided them as charlatans and said that Cato was amazed that one haruspex did not laugh when he met another. He also said that Julius Caesar was warned by a haruspex not to go to Africa before the winter solstice but he ignored this advice and his arrival prevented his enemies from joining together. Pompey placed great trust in divination by means of entrails and portents, but, asked Cicero, what assistance had they been to him? Nevertheless, haruspices continued to exist because in the fourth century AD. Theodosius declared that if the imperial palace was to be struck by lightning they were to be consulted.

There were two other colleges of lesser standing. One comprised first 2, then 10, then up to 15 men (*duroviri, decemviri* and *quindecimviri sacris faciundis*). Their main duty was to consult the Sibylline Books, a traditional collection of Greek verses reputed to be the frenzied utterances of the Sybil of Cumae. These had been given to Tarquinius Priscus and were kept in the Temple of Jupiter on the Capitol. The Senate ordered them to be consulted on religious matters, especially when it was necessary to determine whether a foreign cult should be allowed in Rome or when the Romans were faced with a crisis. The other was the College of Epulones, about 10 men who supervised the feasts and public banquets held during festivals and at the games.

In addition there were other groups, such as the Arval Brethren who celebrated the festival of the goddess Dea Dia in May, an ancient agricultural cult and the Luperci who celebrated the Lupercalia on 15 February, a peculiar ritual which Plutarch thought was a festival of purification as it included a sacrifice of a goat and a dog. Mark Anthony took part in one Lupercalia in 44 BC and offered a diadem to Caesar who was sitting on the Rostra. Twice Caesar refused it to the applause of the crowd, noting that very few applauded when it was offered to him. Thus, said Plutarch, the experiment (of trying to make to make Caesar imperial) failed.

The College of the Fetiales comprised 20 men who conducted relations with Rome's neighbours arranging treaties or declaring war. If any neighbouring territory was hostile, four men were sent to demand their intentions or if there had been some outrage to demand retribution. If negotiations did not prove satisfactory one of the fetiales would throw a spear towards the enemy to demean his power. Later, as this primitive ritual seemed inappropriate, the Romans replaced the fetiales by ambassadors. The ritual was then reduced to throwing a spear into the ground in front of the Temple of Bellona, the goddess of war. This custom

A statue in the Forum Romanum believed to
be one of the head vestal virgins

long survived as Marcus Aurelius performed this in
AD 178 before campaigning on the Danube frontier.

These priesthoods were exclusively male. The only
priestesses were the Vestal Virgins, dedicated to the
worship of Vesta, goddess of the hearth, originally
four and later six in number, and chosen by the kings
in accordance to the decrees of Numa. They had to
be age 6–10, have both parents living, be physically
unblemished and a virgin. They were shown to the
Pontifex Maximus, who said, 'I take you Amata
(beloved one).' Their crucial role was not to let the
sacred fire go out, for this represented the goddess
who had no image. The temple contained the statue
of Pallas Athene, which Aeneas was reputed to have
brought from Troy. The fire and the statue assured
the safety of Rome and there could be disaster if the
fire went out. Only on 1 March was it ritually relit by
the primitive means of rubbing two sticks together.

For the first 10 years a girl learned the rites, in
the second 10 she performed them and in the third
10 she taught them to the younger ones. After that
she could marry but many stayed, preferring to live
in honourable retirement. They were held in great
honour but any transgression could be punished by
whipping or in extreme cases they were carried on
a funeral bier and placed in an underground cell at
the Porta Collina. To avoid this sentence some were
urged to commit suicide.

HONOURS PAID TO THE GODS

There were a number of ways in which the gods were
worshipped and placated – prayers, vows, obligations
and, above all, sacrifices. State ceremonies demanded
living victims. In the early eras these might be
human, but animals – pigs, sheep, goats and oxen –
quickly replaced them. Cicero detailed what should
be chosen. Male animals were sacrificed to male gods

and female animals to female goddesses; black animals for the underworld gods, white animals for the heavenly gods. Size also had to be considered: a bull for Jupiter, a sheep for Juno. Killing of animals could be a difficult and bloody business. R.M. Ogilvie has drawn a parallel to 160,000 messy, mooing cows being led though Whitehall and butchered in the precincts of Westminster Abbey. This was how Caligula's accession, according to Suetonius, was celebrated on the Capitol over three months. Ogilvie suggested that animals were necessary because they were essentially active. The gods were gods of activity and activity has to be renewed and sustained. For humble households the heart, liver and entrails, the vital parts of the body, were acceptable.

The animal was led to the temple where elaborate rituals tool place. Flour was sprinkled on the animal's horns and wine poured over the head. When the moment came the priest called for silence, '*favete linguis*' (check your tongues) and asked the worshippers 'Do I strike?' If the answer was 'Yes', his acolyte stunned the animal and a *cultrarius* cut the throat allowing some of the blood to pour onto the ground; the rest was collected in jars. A haruspex was at hand to study the entrails. Meat could then be distributed in order of precedence, first to the priests, then to senators and important guests. It might be distributed to the poor or sold to butchers, who would also make use of the blood for blood puddings, which they knew would sell for a good price. Temples had to be provided with good drains for the blood; an ox has two gallons. Slaves cleared the resulting mess of blood and faeces.

Less bloody and probably less exciting were the prayers and vows offered. Livy recorded three kinds of prayers: some sought favourable portents, some avoided evil and some gave praise for services rendered. Magistrates appealed to the gods with set prayers helped by three attendants. One dictated the prayer from a script, another checked to see that he was speaking correctly, the

Temple of Vespasian, Pompeii. The temple is now believed to be older, dating to the reign of Augustus, but it was certainly dedicated to the Imperial Cult

Relief depicting a sacrifice on the altar in front of the Temple of Vespasian. On the left is a priest with his toga pulled over his head; on the right a bull is being led forward to be sacrificed

third enforced silence. A flautist might play so that nothing but the prayer was heard. If prayers were not exact, they had to be repeated or disaster might ensue and prayers not answered.

Vows did not need be offered at an altar. They could be written on wax tablets left in a shrine. If made to a water deity they or suitable votive objects were cast into a stream, a river or a well. Models of parts of bodies in need of healing were left at healing shrines. Victorious generals dedicated spoils of war. Livy gave an example to show that less expensive gifts were accepted. The consul, Lucius Papirius, fighting the Samnites in 292 BC, vowed to Jupiter Victor that if he defeated them he would present the god with a cup of mead before he drank wine himself. Jupiter, amazed at his presumption, accepted this and the enemy was defeated.

Farmers had to be particularly careful. Cato gave instructions on what must be done when thinning a grove. First a pig should be sacrificed, Then a prayer should be exactly spoken so that it covered all eventualities.

Whether thou be god or goddess to whom this grove is dedicated, as it is thy right to receive a sacrifice of a pig for the thinning of this sacred grove, and to this intent, whether I or one at my bidding do it, may it be rightly done. To this end, in offering this pig to thee I humbly beg that thou will be gracious and merciful to me and my household, and to my children. Wilt thou deign to receive this pig which I offer to thee to this end.

A similar prayer was made when ground was tilled with the words added, 'for the sake of doing this work.' That prayer had to be made each day as long as the work continued.

Areas and people could be purified, thus freeing them from hostile demons. Priests processed round the area, then made a sacrifice or said prayers. February was the usual month when purifications took place and 27 February was the day of the Amburbium when a ceremony to purify Rome was held. A pig, a sheep and an ox were led in procession round the boundaries of the city and then sacrificed.

The Temple of Fortuna Virilis, Rome dating to c.80–70 BC in the Forum Boarium replaced an earlier one. This temple is now suggested to have been dedicated to the harbour god, Portunus, because in antiquity the temple was just inside the harbour area. The temple survived because it was converted into a church dedicated to St Mary around AD 872

One popular way in which the gods could be honoured was to hold games. Most were preceded by a procession, which included animals, musicians and the contestants. The games might be held annually or presented as a votive offering by a man seeking high office or by a victorious general. Sometimes the games took the form of stage shows, a play by an eminent playwright, a chariot race and gladiatorial displays. Livy said that the first time an athletic contest was given it was by Marcus Fulvius Nobilior after his victory over Aetolia in 189 BC. These spectacles became more elaborate as each donor of the games tried to outdo a previous one.

Suetonius gave a description of the elaborate games given by Julius Caesar in 65 BC when he was an aedile but the Senate, wary of the gladiators Caesar had hired, restricted the number which people were allowed to keep in Rome. Sparticus's slave revolt of 73–71 BC still remained in Roman memories. Cicero thought that the games given by Pompey in 55 BC in honour of Venus Victrix at the opening of his theatre were the most magnificent in the history of man and that he could not imagine that future eras would ever show their like. Those given in the empire surpassed them but increasingly, although their purpose was to honour the gods, they reflected the honour of the emperors.

EMPEROR WORSHIP

It was therefore not surprising that emperors should be regarded as gods or even declared they *were* gods. Julius Caesar had declared that the Julian family was descended from Venus, the mother of Aeneas who had fled from Troy and ultimately founded the Roman nation. This he had emphasised by building a temple to Venus Genetrix (Venus the Mother). He had also been granted his own *flamen*, had been given four triumphs and held all the great offices of state. According to Suetonius, after his assassination, on the first day of the games which Octavian, Caesar's great-nephew and adopted son was celebrating in honour of Venus Genetrix, a comet appeared and shone for seven days. The spectators immediately took this as a sign that Caesar had joined the heavenly pantheon and Octavian did not correct this view. In January 42 BC the Senate declared Julius Caesar to be *divus Julius*.

For the next two centuries most emperors were deified after their deaths, a practice common in Egypt and Asia Minor. The Egyptians regarded the pharaohs as gods. Persian emperors were

perceived as gods and when Alexander the Great finally defeated Darius III in 331 BC it was considered he would assume the godhead.

Although Augustus never claimed divinity in his lifetime, the Senate granted him special honours including one of people pouring a libation to him at public and private banquets, an honour usually reserved for deities. In 27 BC Octavius assumed the name Augustus. Later the historian Florus declared this raised him to the title of a god and he was, after all, the son of a god. Ovid had no doubts about this. In his *Fasti*, speaking of Augustus's house on the Palatine, he allotted one third to Phoebus (Apollo), a second to Venus and a third to Augustus himself, claiming 'a single house holds three gods'. Augustus also reorganised the worship of the Lares Compitales integrating them with his own Genius so that Ovid could proclaim 'In every city there are a thousand Lares and the Genius ... now the *vici* (districts) worship three divinities.' On his funeral pyre an ex-praetor swore that he had seen Augustus's spirit soaring to Heaven through the flames. It was therefore inevitable that he should be declared *divus* and Tacitus recorded his deifications and a temple decreed in his honour. Augustus had not prevented dedications to his divinity in other parts of the empire such as Pergamum and Nicomedia, and later Dio Cassius, in the third century AD, commented that this was where the practice of emperor worship started.

Suetonius said that Tiberius specifically forbade any attempt to deify himself, but Claudius was given a princely funeral and officially deified. From then on other emperors were deified, some such as Caligula, Nero and Commodus demanding this status in their lifetime. Commodus not only identified himself with Mercury but also with Hercules. Some such as Vespasian showed scepticism; he remarked when dying, 'Alas I think I am becoming a god.' The Imperial Cult, however, had a political purpose. It promoted loyalty especially in the provinces and amongst the military. It was not until the third century that Aurelian changed the format. Instead of the emperor being divine, Aurelian changed it to the emperor being divine (or ruling) by the grace of God. Whether he implied the Christian god or the Sun God to whose worship he was devoted is unclear, but Constantine accepted he was God's vice-regent on earth, not a god himself.

HOUSEHOLD RELIGION

Ordinary householders could participate in state religion, but households had their own individual deities although Cicero emphasised that these should be in agreement with those of the state. The protective deities of the household were the Lares and Penates. The Lares protected the family; the Penates protected the store cupboard (*penus*) to ensure plenty. Houses had a household shrine (*lararium*) usually placed in the atrium. The one in the House of the Vettii at Pompeii has a painted wall behind it showing two Lars, each holding a *rhyton* (drinking horn), standing either side of the Genius or guardian spirit of the house and individual members of the family, especially the *paterfamilias*. He wears a toga with the folds pulled over the head in the stance of a priest at the moment of sacrifice. Underneath glides a serpent moving towards a small altar; a serpent usually represented fertility.

Other deities who protected the household included Vesta, whose worship was necessary to keep a fire alight because of the problem of rekindling it and also to prevent it getting out of hand and burning down the house. A small piece of salted cake was thrown into the fire for

Bronze figurine of a Lar found at
Felmingham Hall, England

her use. A door had its own deities and had to be guarded against evil spirits. The door was the
home of Janus who faced two ways. Janus Patulcius guarded the opening of the door. Janus
Clusivius guarded its closing. Lamentinus protected the threshold and Cardea the hinge. A new
bride was carried over the threshold so that she might not stumble and thus bring bad luck. She
then had to make a gift to the Lares of the household and the Lares Compitales, who protected
the neighbourhood.

Bronze figurines represented these deities. Each household had its particular deity. Martial,
who had lived in Rome since AD 64, returned to his native Spain in AD 98. When he left his
beloved country property he hoped that the new owners would honour his household deities
and keep their rites. These included Jupiter the Thunderer, the woodland god Silvanus,

Bronze figurine of a Genius found at
Cricklade, England

Mars, Flora and the virgin goddess Diana. He commented on the altars 'built by the bailiff's
unpractised hand' which may imply that as well as a *lararium* he had altars built on other parts
of his property.

Usually the *paterfamilias* made offerings. These could be modest. In one of his Odes Horace
mentioned ritual salt and spelt dancing in the flames to Vesta. He added that during a main meal
a small piece of food was thrown into the fire so that the Lars could consume it. Occasionally
women made offerings. In Plautus's play *The Pot of Gold* the prologue is spoken by the *Lar
Familiaris* who says he had protected the dwelling for many years from the time of the grandsire
to the present owner. But he has been neglected so the daughter prayed to him constantly
giving him garlands and daily offerings of incense and wine.

ENTRY OF FOREIGN CULTS

Roman religion was tolerant of other cults which were brought to Rome. Roman beliefs were akin to those of their Latin and Etruscan neighbours and the Etruscans had absorbed many of the Greek deities. Minerva was both a warrior goddess and a goddess of crafts; Mercury was a god of traders. Venus's character developed from being a protector of gardens; Fortuna, a goddess of both good and ill luck, was adopted as an agricultural deity worshipped at Praeneste. Both the Etruscans and the Greeks saw them having human characteristics and foibles. The pantheon of gods was a family akin to a human family and thus understandable. Statues gave the gods particular identifications; Jupiter held a thunderbolt, Mercury a winged cap or winged heels, Mars, originally a fertility deity, was linked with the Greek Ares becoming an armed warrior god.

The Temple of Jupiter on the Capitol was built first by the Etruscan kings and dedicated to the Etruscan deities, Tinia, Uni and Menrva who emerged in the Roman pantheon as Jupiter, Juno and Minerva. Soon Jupiter became the deity who presided over the whole state as Jupiter Optimus Maximus. Varro said that from 753 BC the Romans worshipped their gods without images but within 150 years images had been created, thus removing fear but adding error. In 399 BC the Sibylline Books had instructed that images of three pairs of gods should be placed on coaches with tables laid with food and drink in front of them, thus emphasising their likeness to mankind.

Greek deities entered Roman religion from the Greek cities in the south of Italy and from Greece itself. In some cases, for example that of Hercules, the cult may have been a private one, for Hercules was the Greek hero Heracles whose 12 labours had made him famous. By the late fourth century he had been accepted into the state religion to become protector of merchants. When plague broke out in Rome in 433 BC Apollo was called on as a healing god, but his functions also included prophecy and the care of flocks and herds. When another pestilence came in 292 BC the Sibylline Books were consulted and advised that the healing god, Aesculapius, should be brought from Epidaurus. An expedition was sent and returned with a serpent in the guise of the god. When the boat arrived at Rome the serpent slipped over the side and crawled onto Tiber Island. A temple and healing shrine were built there to the god.

The Senate who controlled the interpretation of the Sibylline Books often admitted foreign gods into Rome. These included gods from Asia and Africa. When the Books were consulted during the invasion of Italy by Hannibal, they said he could only be defeated if the Idaean Mother known as Cybele came to Rome. In 204 BC she was brought in the form of a sacred black stone, which was placed in the Temple of Victory on the Palatine. Cybele became the first foreign deity to be installed within the city where she was given the name of Magna Mater (Great Mother). She was welcomed with a banquet and soon an annual festival and games, the Megalensia, was established. The games were held in the Circus Maximus, which the goddess could survey from her temple where she had been represented as a woman in a chariot drawn by lions.

In admitting this goddess the Romans gained more than they had anticipated, for the cult of the goddess was organised by oriental eunuch priests called Galli. They processed with her image, whipping and cutting themselves, and, as Ovid said, 'thumping their hollow drums and clashing cymbal upon cymbal'. Dionysius of Halicarnassus said that Roman citizens were

Statue of Dionysus from Pompeii.
(Museo Archeologico Nazionale,
Naples)

forbidden to march in the procession, still less to become priests where they would have to undergo castration. The cult, however, gained popularity. In the empire dining clubs were established in honour of the goddess and it was no longer eunuchs who could become priests.

Restrictions were also placed on the cult of Dionysus who entered Rome under the guise of Bacchus. Bacchic rites had been confined to women and to daylight hours, but as the cult had the appeal of wine, feasting and drunkenness, men soon joined and according to Livy the cult became notorious for the promiscuous mating of freeborn men and women. The Senate tried to curb these excesses in 186 BC on the grounds of conspiracy. Bacchic groups were to be limited to five and application had to be made to a quorum of no less than 100 in the Senate for any larger gathering. All new shrines were to be destroyed. It might have been curtailed but it was not suppressed and the cult continued in secret.

Egyptian cults included those of Isis brought in the first century BC. She was popular with women as she protected them in childbirth. Apuleius in *The Golden Ass* addressed her as 'Holy and eternal saviour of mankind who bountifully nurtures us, protector of men on sea and land; you drive away the storm winds of life and stretch out your rescuing hands with which you unwind the threads of fate.' The cult of Isis was quickly followed by that of Osiris who was linked with Serapis, whose fertility symbol was a corn modius on his head.

These cults appealed because they were personal and satisfied an emotional need, even promising a better life after death. They had an element of mystery about them especially in their ritual as worshippers were sworn to secrecy. One cult becoming very popular in the second century AD was that of Mithras, a Persian god. Two divine powers were in opposition: Ahuramazda, lord of light and life; Ahriman, lord of darkness and death. Ahuramazda created Mithras from a rock, making him intermediary with mankind and its struggle with the forces of evil. Mithraic reliefs show Mithras dressed in a tunic and Phrygian cap slaying a bull, the creation of Ahuramazda, which had been tracked by a raven. From the blood sprang the vine of life; from the spinal cord came wheat and from the body came the plants useful to man. A dog and serpent, servants of Ahriman lick the blood but to no avail as it spreads over the earth. Mithras had thus overcome the powers of darkness and was carried by the chariot of the sun to the Heavens.

Ceremonies took place in mithraea either underground or in buildings with no windows. A mithraeum was found under the lower levels of the Church of San Clemente in Rome; the foundation of a large ground-based temple was discovered in London. Initiates passed from one rank to the next through seven grades – Raven, Hidden One, Soldier, Lion, Persian and Sun Runner. Father, the highest grade, presided over ceremonies. When a group became too large another was formed which was probably why the authorities did not suppress the cult. Another reason could be that Mithraism, with its stern demands on its devotees to become morally pure and its vision of the protection of mankind was popular with the military and merchants, two groups whom the authorities respected.

When the Romans extended into the Celtic areas of Europe they found themselves confronted by a large number of Celtic cults. The Celts did not display their deities in human form. Their deities were linked to natural phenomena – trees, groves, water thunder and lightning. The triad was sacred – the three Mother Goddesses, the three *Genii Cucullati* (the Hooded Ones). These gods were incorporated into Roman religion, but not brought to Rome. The *interpretatio Romana* linked the Celtic deities to Roman ones so that Belatucadrus and Cocidius, the Celtic

Statue of Mithras slaying the Sacred Bull, Roman, second century AD. (British Museum)

gods of war were syncretised with Mars who might also be syncretised with Teutates or Taranis. Taranis the greatest of the gods was syncretised with Jupiter. Some gods such as the smith god had a name which eluded the Romans, so he became absorbed into the Roman Vulcan.

Soldiers stationed far from Rome, especially those from the provinces, were at home with these gods and with the Teutonic ones so that dedications exist to Mars Thincsus and the goddesses Alaisiagae. The Romans allowed the Celts to build their own form of temple with a raised *cella* surrounded by a veranda and to worship their gods in their own way. The one area they did suppress was Druidism, partly because they suspected it was responsible for human sacrifices and partly because it challenged Roman political power. Suetonius said that both Tiberius and Claudius suppressed the Druidic priesthood and the last effective remnants in Britain were extinguished when the Roman governor of Britain, Suetonius Paulinus invaded Anglesey in AD 60 where the Druids had gathered for a last stand.

The influx of foreign cults into Rome continued. In the early second century AD Juvenal expressed his exasperation,

I cannot stand a Greekified Rome. Yet how few of our dregs come from Greece. The Syrian Orontes for a long time has polluted the Tiber bringing its language and customs.

JUDAISM

One group of people baffled the Romans; Tacitus noted

> Jews conceive of only one god and that they regard as impious anyone who makes images of god in the likeness of men. The supreme and eternal being is to them incapable of representation and without end. They therefore erect no statues to him in their cities, still less in their temples, nor is their honour given to Caesar.

Thus Jews could not be reconciled with the Roman worship of numerous deities and certainly not with emperor worship. There was a permanent presence of Jews in Rome and many other cities throughout the empire. The Jewish historian Josephus said that Julius Caesar granted the Jews in Rome exemption from a ban on religious assembles and allowed them to collect money and have communal meals. In 43 BC the Roman commander in Asia Minor granted exemption from military service to Jews living in that area. Still, Jews living in Sardinia were punished for refusing military service.

The Romans were never certain of the loyalty of the Jews to the state. Tiberius and Claudius expelled most of them from Rome. Problems in Judea eventually led to the Jewish War and the conquest of Jerusalem in AD 70 when the Temple was destroyed and the sacred vessels taken in triumph to Rome. A second revolt in Judea in AD 132–135 was equally brutally crushed with the Jews being driven out of the Jerusalem. Hadrian renamed Jerusalem 'Aelia' after his family name and Judea was named Palestine.

CHRISTIANITY

If there was a problem with the Jews there was an even greater one with the Christians. Christianity seems to have arrived in Rome by the reign of Claudius. Suetonius recorded that Claudius expelled the Jews who constantly made disturbances in the name of 'Chrestus'. Nero made them scapegoats after the fire of 64 AD and Tacitus referred to them being 'loathed for their vices'. They were accused of being a clandestine organisation and their refusal to participate in emperor worship was potentially treasonable. Pliny, when governor of Bithynia, wrote to Trajan saying he proposed to ask these people three times if they were Christians. If they denied it they were to be released, but if they persisted in saying they were he would have them executed. If they denied it, however, they were to make an offering of incense to Trajan's image, which Pliny had cunningly placed amongst those of other gods. Trajan, however, said that Christians were not in general to be persecuted; each case was to be treated on its own merits, and this does seem to have been the case until the time of Decius.

Although rumours of conspiracies, rabble rousing and secret rituals were common, Tertullian writing in the early third century stated and refuted accusations against Christians. Systematic persecution was instituted in the third century by the emperor Decius who decreed that all inhabitants of the Roman Empire, except the Jews, must worship the Roman gods and himself as lord and god, believing that was the only way to unite what was becoming an increasingly

The Emperor Decius

chaotic empire. The crucial test was again to be the offering of incense and the pouring of a libation; certificates could be given to show this had been done.

Relief came in AD 312 when Constantine converted to Christianity after the Battle of the Milvian Bridge, believing that a vision of the sign of a cross in the sky ensured victory and ordering his soldiers to put the Chi-Rho monogram on their shields. His Edict of Milan granted toleration and in AD 325 at the Council of Nicaea, Christianity became the *de facto* religion of the empire. There were still eras of persecution, notably in AD 361–363 when Julian revived pagan faiths but the eventual triumph of the Christian faith was assured and it spread throughout the empire.

It is possible that Christianity triumphed because the stoicism and bravery of the Christians under bouts of persecution influenced others. Tacitus said, referring to Nero's persecution, that there arose pity due to the impression that these people were sacrificed not for the welfare of the state but to the ferocity of one man. Christianity also promised hope of immortality and emphasised spiritual nature against the materialism of much of Roman life. It is also possible that faith in the Roman gods decreased during the breakdown in society during the latter day of the empire and a static official religion failed to control more innovative religions which became identified with individuals' specific needs. Gradually Christianity became the accepted religion, but after the empire declined Christianity was faced with a different kind of paganism.

8

ENTERTAINMENT

R ome was a spectacle in itself and her citizens were always alert for anything that would relieve the monotony. Apart from entertainments taking place at theatres, amphitheatres and stadia, much was provided free in the street. The open doors of the Senate House allowed proceedings to be seen and spectators noted the arrival and departure of the senators and petitioning clients. There were chances to participate in public feasts, as well as viewing the numerous quarrels, fights and general mayhem that could arise in a crowded city. Speeches were often made from the Rostrum in the Forum. Suetonius recorded the visit of Tiridates, an Armenian prince, to Nero. The weather was cloudy but this did not deter Nero. The Praetorian Guard marched in full armour round the temples of the Forum while Nero watched from the Rostrum. Tiridates prostrated himself before Nero, who stretched out his hand to raise him to his feet. Further supplications were made at the theatre and on the Capitol in front of huge crowds.

The public also held their own meetings, often rowdy and boisterous, but which Cicero praised as being the best way in which opinions and wishes of the citizens could be clearly expressed. A *contio* was a formally constituted meeting summoned by a magistrate where discussions could take place. This meeting conveyed information and took soundings of opinion preparatory to calling an assembly (*comitia*) at which citizens could vote on topics already discussed in a *contio*. Politicians took advantage of this. In 63 BC Cicero denounced Cataline in the Senate for corruption, then held a public meeting to explain what had happened and to condemn a conspiracy.

TRIUMPHAL PROCESSIONS

Triumphal processions controlled by the Senate were given to victorious generals and at least 320 are known to have taken place up to the reign of Vespasian, some lasting over several days. A general had to have conducted a legitimate war, secured enemy territory and killed at least 5,000 enemies. Processions wound their way through the city, finally going along the Via Sacra through the Forum to the Temple of Jupiter. Emperors often granted themselves one.

When Nero returned from Greece in AD 67 he staged a pseudo-triumph. Riding in a chariot, arrayed in a purple robe and a Greek cloak decorated with gold stars, he was followed by groups of young men whom he had bribed to shout his triumph. Along the route victims were slain, the streets were sprinkled with perfume and, best of all, he had sweetmeats showered on him, which, no doubt, went into the crowds.

The procession of Titus and Vespasian in AD 71 after the fall of Jerusalem was a more genuine one. Josephus said it was impossible to give an adequate description of the spectacle. The procession included floats and tableaux reflecting events from the Jewish War, 700 Jewish captives and all the treasures taken from the Temple in Jerusalem including huge bronze lamps, the bronze table and the Menorah. These were permanently recorded on the Arch of Titus. To make it clear who was victorious, Simon, son of Giora, who had fought against the Romans, was dragged out of the procession, beaten and executed. The rest of the day was devoted to a public feast. Septimius Severus, however, was so crippled with gout that he had to forgo a triumph because he could not stand up in the triumphal chariot.

FESTIVAL DAYS

Numerous festival days provided processions. Dionysus of Helicarnassus describes that of 15 July when a cavalry parade commemorated the help given by Castor and Pollux at the Battle of Lake Regillus. Saturnalia, when slaves and masters changed places, was celebrated with a banquet which anyone could attend. Seneca recorded, with some disapproval, the noise of a rejoicing city. Pliny the Younger preferred to retreat into a soundproof bedroom. Public feasts on festival days were given throughout the year organised by the College of Epulones. Most were for senators but food was also provided for ordinary citizens and in a city where news travelled fast, many would arrive to take their share. Festivals were also celebrated in the theatres and amphitheatres.

BATHING AND THE BATHS

A minor entertainment but one that was appreciated, was that taken at the public baths. Going to the public baths provided social activity, a means of meeting friends and hearing the latest news. Some Roman houses did have private baths and guests used them to bathe before dinner. During the republic some wealthy citizens built a bathhouse by the side of their house, which the public could use for a fee.

The earliest public baths in Rome had been built by the side of the Appian Way in the third century BC but their number increased during the empire. Agrippa on the Campus Martius built the first. Later emperors from Nero to Constantine realised the value of providing these public amenities, which were built on a monumental scale. The Baths of Caracalla covered 100,000m². Those of Diocletian served 3000 bathers at one time and were used until the sixth century AD.

Bathing was not only a social activity. Cleanliness, removal of body hair, trimming of hair and beards and physical exercise was part of the civilising process. In this way citizens

A public communal latrine built opposite to the Forum Baths, Ostia, and included as part of the renovation of the baths in the fourth century. Martial mocked Vacerra who dallied in similar baths, sitting for hours, not relieving himself, but hoping to cadge an invitation to dinner

enhanced their status. Bathing separated a civilised individual from an uncouth barbarian, hence the encouragement to build public baths throughout the empire provided either by the town council or by private citizens. Forts, even in the far distant parts of the empire, provided them both to satisfy the army, and as a way of civilising auxiliary provincial troops.

Bathing had its own ritual. Romans usually bathed naked so men and women bathed separately at different times of the day; they could wear a simple tunic. Towels, oils and strigils were used to scrape off the grime from their bodies. Many people had their personal slave in attendance; others might hire them. Juvenal commented on a woman who bathed by night and had her equipment taken there by slaves. Hadrian, on one visit, noticed an old man scraping himself on a wall because he was too poor to have a slave. He promptly gave him several slaves and money for their keep. On a subsequent visit he saw several men scraping themselves on wall. He merely commanded them to line up and scrape each other.

Bathers undressed in the *apodyterium*, placing their clothes in niches or leaving them with attendants. They might exercise in the *palaestra* beforehand, after which the sweat was scraped off with the strigil. They next went into the *tepidarium*, a warm room that could have a bath of warm water in it. Beyond that, the *caldarium* had a bath with waist-high hot water. Here, they sweated to open the pores. Thick sandals were necessary because of the hot floors. The bathers cooled in the *tepidarium* before finishing in the *frigidarium* where they bathed in the cold pool. They might have a sauna in the dry heat *laconicum*, spend time being massaged with perfumed oils or swim in the *natatio*, a large outdoor pool.

Bathing establishments could be both expensive to construct and to maintain, especially as they consumed a great deal of fuel to heat the water, yet bathing not only indicated Roman civilised habits but also provided work for large numbers of people. They also served as clubs with their facilities including eating places and latrines. Some baths were linked with healing deities as was that at Bath, where the temple of Sulis Minerva was a dominant feature. By the end of the empire a different attitude had emerged which regarded bathing as sexual gratification. The Christians therefore promoted the healing springs of saints rather than the cleanliness of the body and the large thermal establishments fell into decay.

THEATRES

The first theatres were wooden stages easily portable and moved by the players from town to town. Vitruvius in the first century AD said that they were being built in his day in great numbers. These had an acting arena, perhaps the ground or a low platform, a wall behind it and a wing on each side containing dressing rooms. The Greeks already had permanent theatres, some in Sicily, and this would have influenced later Roman building. Livy recorded Greek actors performing in Rome over a 10-day period in 186 BC during the games given by Marcus Fulvius.

Wooden stages were erected in the Forum for theatrical performances during games held in conjunction with religious festivals. Livy said that the censor M. Antonius Lepidus contracted for a theatre and proscaenium building at the dedication of the Temple of Apollo in 179 BC, probably a temporary building used only for performances in honour of the god. In 167 BC the Praetor Lucius Anicius, after conquering the Illyrians, put on games in honour of this victory. He erected a huge stage in the Forum and brought in famous flute players to entertain the crowd, but told them that they were not playing well. They did not understand what exactly he meant until a lictor explained that they should compete with each other. They then played with vigour. The melee increased when four prizefighters attacked them. Polybius said that if he had tried to record the scene some of his readers might think he was making it up, but it was hugely popular.

The first attempt to build a permanent theatre in Rome was in 154 BC near the Palatine Hill, but a former consul, P. Cornelius Nasica, who was against the work on moral grounds, persuaded the Senate to demolish it three years later. The debris was auctioned. The result was, however, that temporary stages became even more elaborate. In 99 BC the aedile Claudius Pulcher created so real a painted background that, according to Pliny the Elder, cranes were deceived into trying to alight on the roof tiles. About 69 BC Quintus Lutatius Catulus, when celebrating the dedication of the rebuilt Temple of Jupiter added the luxury of a velum, an awning to protect spectators from the sun. An awning is depicted on a painting of the amphitheatre at Pompeii. Lucretius mentioned yellow, red and dark purple awnings fluttering in the winds.

Increasingly elaborate decoration was added to theatres. Valerius Maximus mentioned decorations in gold, silver and ivory. Pliny the Elder spoke with awe of a theatre constructed on the order of the aedile Marcus Scaurus in 58 BC, which surpassed everything built before. This consisted of a stage arranged in three storeys with 360 columns, the lower ones of marble, the

second row of glass and the third row of gilded planks. It had 3000 statues and accommodated 80,000 people. Gaius Curio trumped this in 52 BC with two theatres each balanced on a revolving pivot. Plays could be given in each of them as they faced back to back. They could be swivelled round to face each other thus producing an amphitheatre to hold gladiatorial fights. Pliny said, however, that the seats were rickety and the pivots unreliable because the two halves might swing round with the spectators still seated on them.

All these theatres were temporary. The first permanent one in Rome was built by Pompey in 55 BC as part of the elaborate triumph he awarded himself for his victories in Syria and Judea. Nothing remains of Pompey's theatre today but it probably resembled the Theatre of Marcellus. Caesar had begun this but ironically he was assassinated in Pompey's theatre where the Senate was temporarily sitting before the new Senate House was completed. Augustus completed the building of the theatre in 13 BC and dedicated it to his nephew and son-in-law Marcellus. Part of the impressive façade survives and this became the model for succeeding theatres.

Vitruvius laid down instructions for the site and building of a theatre. The site should be as healthy as possible because citizens and their wives and children remained motionless with pleasure, and might be exposed to unhealthy winds or the blazing sun. This comment seems to indicate that there was no segregation of families although special seats were reserved for the senators. Examples of bone and ivory tickets found at Rome, Pompeii and elsewhere show that, as in a modern theatre, seating arrangements were precise.

The curving exterior of the Theatre of Marcellus, Rome. The lower arches gave access to the seating in the lower areas and to staircases leading to the upper areas

Theatre building took place throughout the empire. Some theatres were the gift of citizens or of the emperor, such as the theatre at Orange in Gaul. This theatre, which dates from AD 10–25, has the best extant postscaenium wall; Louis XIV called it 'the finest wall in my kingdom.' The *fronscaenae* was decorated with marble columns and statues and was protected by a large lean-to roof. The stagehands and actors were able to move between the panelled ceiling and the tiled roof as well as through passages inside the wall. Their dressing rooms were built on both sides of the stage. A curtain was raised and lowered by an ingenious arrangement of cables, hoists and counterweights thus concealing the actors from the spectators.

The rows of seats built in a semicircle followed Vitruvius's suggestion that the construction of a theatre was easier if it was built into the hillside. However, many theatres had built-up seating. Each set of rows was divided into *cunei* (wedge-shapes) by flights of steps rising from the orchestra to the upper levels. An inscription at Thugga mentions *designatores* and *monitores cancelli*. The former showed people to their seats and the latter were prompters. Senators and important officials sat at the front; up to 14 rows could be kept for their use. Some seats had names and numbers carved on them. At Avaricum Biturigum in France an inscription mentions a seat reserved for Gavia Quieta, daughter of the *duumviri* Aemilius Afer. Suetonius said that during Claudius's reign there was trouble in Rome when German envoys took over the senators' seats. Having seen that Parthian and Armenian envoys were sitting with the senators they moved into the same part of the theatre protesting that their merit and rank were

Postscaenium of the Theatre of Orange, Vaucluse, France

Stage and seating of the south theatre at Jerash, Jordan, built in the first century AD. There were 32 tiers of seats accommodating 3000–4000 spectators. Behind the theatre is the oval piazza

not inferior. Claudius, much amused, allowed them to stay. Theatrical performances grew in popularity under the empire. Pompeii had two theatres and the small theatre at Verulamium in Britain was enlarged twice. In that province even the small town of Petuaria (Brough on Humber) had a theatre, probably built of timber, given by the aedile Marcus Ulpius Januarius.

ACTORS

Audiences were entertained by both Greek and Roman plays, some of the most popular being by Plautus and Terence. Horace claimed that many of these plays 'Mighty Rome learns by heart and she views them packed in her crowded theatres.' Rome enjoyed so many plays that almost a third of the year was devoted to them. A thriving acting profession travelled throughout the empire. Comedies were especially popular. A painting in the Naples Museum shows a scene from a comedy with a drunken young man supported by a slave. A musician plays a double pipe and on the left an older man is restrained from moving to hold the young man. Three of these wear masks, a feature copied from the Greeks, which was retained in the Roman theatre.

Some entertainments were dangerous. In Nero's reign during a performance of the story of Icarus and Daedalus the actor playing Icarus fell so close to the emperor that, as he was killed, he spattered him with blood. In Augustus's reign a famous comic actor was whirled in a flying

Three theatre masks which were once part of the stage decoration of the theatre, Ostia

device so quickly that he fell and broke his left shin, but the curtain being pulled up, a roll of thunder and the chorus bursting into song hid the accident.

Many actors were also musicians although Plutarch said that their music was so formless than even a dog could perform it. Music accompanied dancing and general knockabout comedy. Nero gave his own musical performances, locking the gates so that the spectators could not leave. Suetonius alleged that women gave birth, many men feigned death in order to be carried out and others leapt down the outside walls to escape listening and applauding. Nero and other emperors paid for shows. On one occasion Galba allowed the actors to carry away furniture from a burning house and keep it. Good actors could be hired to perform in private households. Some wealthy Romans had performers permanently attached to their staff. Pliny the Younger said that after a dinner he could listen to some music or a comedy; others preferred to have acrobats, clowns and buffoons acting mimes.

Sometimes outspokenness, satirical comments and veiled political allusions went too far. Actors fled from Rome to escape punishment but their popularity allowed for their return. Most actors were slaves or from the lower ranks of society, controlled by a manager. Some were freelance in which case they had to be careful not to offend their patrons. Cicero mentioned that Dionysia, a famous female dancer earned 200,000 sesterces, but that may have included other services rendered. In the republic the law allowed magistrates to punish actors for minor offences but Augustus limited their punishment to misdemeanours during the games or in theatrical performances. Later emperors kept a close watch on what occurred on stage. Marcus Aurelius

tolerated them but Commodus declared some entertainments immoral and exiled the performers. Elagabalus, however, ordered that sexual scenes should be enacted and not feigned. Christians were hostile to the theatre, declaring that some performances were expressions of paganism. The actors often satirised or made hostile remarks about Christianity, frequently parodying its ritual, especially the Virgin birth of Christ and the Eucharist. Later emperors were to regulate these acts.

Roman audiences were always lively and receptive. Performances could be volatile with arguments breaking out between the audience and the actors and amongst the audience themselves. Horace complained about these angry arguments and their demands for animal shows or prizefights in the middle of a performance. Yet many in the audience quoted speeches alongside the actors, appreciated their subtle wit and rose to their feet if a great poet such as Virgil was quoted. Plays could also be performed in temples and sacred places and the fact that plays, mimes, pantomimes and other entertainments continued long after the empire is a tribute to their popularity.

STADIA

Chariot racing, a popular sport in Rome, spread throughout the empire. It took place in a stadium, one of the largest being the Circus Maximus, situated between the Palatine and Aventine Hills, both of which provided a natural viewpoint. According to tradition the first stadium was constructed by Tarquinius Priscus about 600 BC but the first recorded use of it for chariot racing was in the Ludi Romani of 509 BC when Tarquinius Secundus began its rebuilding, probably in wood. It did not take its basic form until the empire. It was an oval 650m by 125m (711 yds by 137 yds) with tiered rows of seats on both sides. Augustus added a box for the imperial court on the Palatine and Claudius provided marble starting gates. During the fire of AD 80 it was destroyed so in AD 103 Trajan replaced the wooden seats with brick faced concrete. It probably held 150,000 people.

There were two other stadia. One was the Circus Flaminius in the Campus Martius; the other was the Circus Maxentius on the Appian Way. Caligula and Nero both had their own private ones and the obelisk from Nero's circus is now placed in front of St Peter's Basilica. Nero was said to be fascinated by chariot races and played every day with ivory chariots on a board. He tried driving a chariot secretly before an audience of slaves and dogs and then began to race in the Campus Martius. Down the middle of the track was a solid barrier with at each end a *meta* or turning post. Two of these still survive in Rome, one in the Piazza del Populo and the other is in the Lateran. On the barrier symbols were displayed altars, statues and shrines.

Chariots were either two wheeled (*biga*) or four wheeled (*quadriga*). The races started from stalls at the flattened end, with the wooden gates all opening at the same time by a mechanism formed of twisted rope. A false start meant the race had to begin again. The track was probably a sandy surface on a firm base. There were usually 12–24 races in a day, although Nero was so fond of them that he added more. Each race took about 10–15 minutes, over seven laps of 1500m (1644 yds) each and the chariots could reach a speed of 64km (40 miles) an hour. They stayed in their own individual lane until the end of the barrier. Then they could move into any position; the closer to the barrier the better chance of winning, but it was more dangerous.

One end of the Circus Maximus, Rome, which occupied the valley between the Palatine and the Aventine

Many charioteers were slaves bought and trained for their prowess. They received a portion of the winnings and if they survived might gain their freedom. Juvenal complained that they earned more in one race than a teacher earned in a year. He adds that Lacerta of the Reds made as much as a 100 lawyers left to their sons. There were few rules and tactics were brutal. Bumping was permitted and the light wood chariots could easily shatter. The only protection for charioteers was leather helmets and coverings for arms and legs. As they tied the reins round their waists to give added force by leaning back, a crash could mean that their horses dragged them on. They carried knives to cut themselves free but had to do this quickly. Pliny the Elder recorded that Corax, a charioteer of the Whites, was thrown out of his chariot but his well-trained horses won the race stopping dead on the finishing line.

Riders were divided into factions denoted by colour. At first there were two colours, red and white, then blue and green were added. Domitian added two further colours, purple and gold, but eventually blue and green absorbed these. Inscriptions from Rome mention careers of charioteers and their factions. Furcas, driver of the Greens, won 53 times and was the first man to win his first race. A driver of the Blues won 47 times with the *quadriga*, was second 131 times and third 146 times; with the *biga* he won nine races and was second and third in eight. He died aged 25.

Fans were fanatical about their teams. Curse tablets have been found wishing ill luck to charioteers and asking that their chariots be broken. Pliny the Elder said that one of the backers of Felix, charioteer of the Reds, flung himself onto his funeral pyre. His rivals claimed he had

Funerary relief showing a *biga* taking part in a chariot race. In the background is a *meta* on a *spina*

A scene on the base supporting the obelisk in the Hippodrome, Istanbul, depicting the Imperial family in their box. Below, kneeling barbarians show their loyalty

just fainted. Pliny the Younger wrote to Calvisius Rufus that the games had not the slightest attraction for him, yet thousands of adult men had a passion for watching galloping horses and drivers standing in chariots. He could account for this if they were attracted by the speed of the chariots and the horse's skill but these men only cared about the racing colours. He was glad that their futile, tedious, monotonous business was not his.

Pliny's was a minority view. In the fourth century AD Ammianus Marcellinus said that the addled, slothful herd longed for the days of chariot racing and rushed to see the sport at top speed as if they would outstrip the chariots. Torn by their conflicts they pass sleepless nights. Ovid gives a different reason for going. As only seating in the lower area was reserved, this was a wonderful opportunity for meeting a lover or obtaining a new one. A long poem by Sidonius Apollinaris, written in the mid-fifth century, gives a thrilling description of a race between four chariots, Blue and White against Red and Green. It also pointed out the dangers:

> Now the enemy pursuing you recklessly, comes across to ram your wheels. The shameless mob of his horses' legs go into the wheels and break the spokes one after the other, until the hub is full of breaking sounds and the rim stops the flying feet. He himself crashes from the collapsing chariot making a mountain of ruin and staining his face with blood. The winner gets silk added to his victory palms; the loser gets a shaggy woollen rug.

NAUMACHIA

Naumachia were mock naval battles. Caesar provided the first one in 46 BC on an excavated lake in the Campus Martius. Augustus staged one in 2 BC with 6000 men, which re-enacted the defeat of the Persians by the Athenians in 480 BC. Tacitus said that Claudius staged one on the Fucine Lake, 60km (37.3 miles) north of Rome, in AD 52 with 100 ships crewed by 19,000 men, all convicted criminals. The banks were patrolled by the Praetorian Guard to stop them escaping.

Domitian created another arena near the Vatican Hill, which became the New Naumachia. Dio Cassius said that during one show a violent storm broke out and almost all the participants and many of the spectators died because Domitian refused to let them leave. It is not certain if naumachia were staged in the Colosseum. Dio Cassius and Suetonius both mention aquatic displays at its opening in AD 80 but it is difficult to see how it was done.

AMPHITHEATRES

The bloodiest but also the most exciting spectacles took place in amphitheatres, the remains of which are found throughout the empire, even in tiny mining villages such as Charterhouse on Mendip in Britain. They were used mainly for gladiatorial contests, animal hunts and spectacles on a grand scale. An amphitheatre was built at Pompeii in AD 70. This was a simple oval structure surrounded by earthen banks on which was placed wooden seating. This seems to have been called a *spectaculum* but by the time of Augustus, the name *amphitheatrum* had been

The amphitheatre at Pompeii, the oldest one known, was constructed in c.80 BC on the orders of C. Quintius Vulgus and M. Porcius. The front seats, which were reserved for magistrates, were reached by their own separate short stairways

adopted. Pliny's story about Curio's two semi-circular theatres, which could be swivelled to form an amphitheatre for gladiatorial contests, may be a mention of an earlier one, but if so it was not permanent.

The first stone amphitheatre in Rome, according to Dio Cassius was built in 28 BC when Statilius Taurus constructed at his own expense a hunting theatre in stone in the Campus Martius and opened it with a gladiatorial contest. This, although intended for wild animal fights, was destroyed but Nero had a wooden one erected in AD 57 on the same site. He widened the entertainment compelling 400 senators and 600 equestrians to fight each other. He is also reported to have held a naval battle in salt water with 'sea monsters', possibly dolphins, swimming in it. Pyrrhic war dances by Greek youths took place while he handed out certificates of Roman citizenship to them.

THE COLOSSEUM

The largest amphitheatre and the one with the most impact was the Colosseum built on the site of Nero's Golden House, begun by Vespasian and completed by Titus. It was 52m (170ft) high, 188m long by 156m wide (617ft long by 512ft), with a capacity of 50,000, but it gained its name not because of its size but because it was situated by a colossal statue of Nero. Suetonius

The Colosseum, Rome

said that Titus dedicated this with most magnificent and costly gladiatorial shows, a sham sea fight and a combat of 5000 beasts of every kind. Dio gave a number of 9000 animals slain, some even killed by women. He added disparagingly that these were not of any prominence. The spectacle lasted for 100 days and many people attended because Titus threw wooden balls into the crowd, variously inscribed with designated articles of clothing, food, gold and silver vessels, even horses, pack animals, cattle and slaves. These could be exchanged for the articles themselves.

The Colosseum was so arranged that, although the social divisions were kept which Augustus had determined, everyone could have a good view. The first level of seating for the senators included a box for the emperor and seating for priests and the Vestal Virgins. This had its own latrines. The second level was for the equestrians, the third and fourth for free born citizens and the highest for women and slaves. Entrance was gained through 76 numbered arcades and tickets indicated entrance, arcade and staircase. Soldiers maintained order. Sprays of perfumes refreshed the spectators and latrines were provided. Shelter from the sun was provided by a huge velarium stretching from masts at the top and worked by sailors from the fleets at Miseneum and Ravenna, who were billeted in Rome. Domitian added chambers under the arena floor to hold animals and trapdoors for them to gain entrance. Scaffolding and other props were also stored there. A huge workforce ran the place and all entertainment was paid for by the emperor and the senators.

Underground passages and cells at the Pozzuoli amphitheatre which would have held wild animals

The Colosseum became the model for other amphitheatres in the provinces including the large ones in North Africa, Spain, Gaul and those attached to the forts. Adverts in Pompeii indicated if there was to be an awning over a particular performance. Aulus Suettius Certus advertised that his gladiators would fight on the last day of May. Attractions were a wild beast show and an awning. Few amphitheatres were built in Greece for the Greeks preferred their customary theatrical performances.

At the Colosseum the programme was usually wild beast shows in the morning, executions of criminals at midday and gladiatorial contests in the afternoon. Huge numbers of wild beasts were killed. These shows had been held before. Cicero said that at games given by Pompey in 55 BC to open his theatre elephants were goaded to fight but the crowd pitied them. There was no feeling of pity during the empire. Animals were brought from every province, the majority coming from North Africa, the wilder and more exotic the better. Nothing was too big or too small, from elephants and crocodiles to foxes and rabbits. Huge cats and bears were the most popular. A vast organisation with trained officials captured them and transported them in cages to Rome. A mosaic at Hippo in North Africa shows animals being driven into an enclosure encircled by a net. One man has fallen and is being attacked by a leopard.

Feeding was costly so the aim was to put them in a show as soon as possible where the noise terrified them, making them wilder as they were urged on by men with whips and goads. Few escaped, unlike the lion in the story of Androcles and the lion recounted by Aulus Gellius. The slaughter was immense. Probus is reported to have sent 100 lions, 200 leopards, 100 lionesses and 300 bears into the arena to be killed. What happened to the bodies is uncertain. Skins could be used for clothing, especially hides in the leather trade. Some bones were discovered in the rooms under the arena. Most were probably thrown into the Tiber, fed to other animals, buried in the surrounding countryside and sold or given away as fresh meat. Josephus said that Caligula's death was mourned by women and youths who had been won over by his theatrical shows, gladiatorial games and the occasional handouts of meat.

CRIMINALS AND PRISONERS

It is uncertain whether Christians were killed in the Colosseum as there is no written evidence for this, although certainly there were martyred in amphitheatres elsewhere. Criminals were a different matter. There were no prisons in Rome for holding long-term prisoners and condemned criminals were sold as slaves, sent to the mines or were dispatched to the amphitheatre to fight wild beasts or each other. Josephus recorded that after the fall of Jerusalem 2500 Jewish captives were put to death. Some criminals were dressed in mythological costumes to die in the manner of a character from legend. Tertullian spoke of prisoners being castrated like the god Attys and being burned in imitation of the fate of Hercules.

Seneca described going to a midday show expecting fun, wit and relaxation. Instead 'in the morning they throw men to the lions and bears; at noon they throw them to the spectators who urge on the slayer to fight another slayer. The outcome of every fight is death and the means are fire and sword.' He added that the executions might be just but he deplored that they were done to excite the spectators.

GLADIATORS

Gladiatorial contests seem to have originated with the Etruscans although frescoes dating to the fourth century BC from the Osco-Samnite tribes south of Naples showed armed combatants at funeral games. The first recorded games in Rome took place in 264 BC when three pairs of gladiators fought at the funeral of Brutus Pera in the Forum Boarium. By the first century BC politicians were putting on gladiatorial shows as a means of boosting their popularity. When Spartacus led 70 gladiators in an escape from the school at Capua, they menaced Rome as they defeated the Roman army on two occasions. Even so the Romans never thought of abolishing gladiatorial contests, but they carefully controlled the training and the games.

Large amphitheatres provided the perfect arenas for these contests and their popularity spread throughout the empire. The shows could be huge. Trajan provided games involving 1000 gladiators fighting in a single show, but outside Rome peripatetic gladiators would be glad to have a few fights in a day.

The name gladiator comes from *gladius*, a sword. This was the usual weapon, but the men carried different weapons and wore a variety of armour. A *murmillo* had a sword, a padded greave, an oblong shield and a defensive helmet. A *thraex* (Thracian) had a small shield, a large helmet, leg guards and a curved sword. A *samnis* (Samnite) had a sword or spear, a vizored helmet, a large shield and one greave. A *hoplomachus* had a straight sword, a small shield, a large crested helmet, a single leg greave and a single arm guard. A *retarius* had a throwing net, trident and dagger and a single arm guard. His aim was to entangle his opponent in the net, then strike with the trident. Suetonius said that Caligula supported the Thracians so much that he curtailed the armour of their opponents.

A Gladiator's helmet

Gladiators paraded in the arena before fighting and greeted the emperor or the sponsor of the games with the words, '*Ave, imperator, morituri te salutamus*' 'Hail, emperor, we who are about to die, salute you'. Individual combats usually lasted about 10–15 minutes, with several taking place at one time, mostly consisting of thrusting and parrying. Fights were not necessarily to the death. Gladiators were expensive to train and overseers preferred to keep their men alive. Advertisements in Pompeii promoted men with 20–40 fights and tombstones recorded even more contests. A defeated man would raise a finger of his left hand to appeal to the crowd and, it is suggested, that the emperor or the spectators would give the thumbs up for approval and the thumbs down for disapproval, gestures which depended on the fighting spirit and courage shown by the combatants. However, whether in fact the thumb was moved up or down is unclear in the historical record; it may have been angled towards the judge to indicate striking a deadly blow, or may have been hidden in the fist or held horizontally, but whether to show a positive or negative outcome is unknown.

Prizes included wreaths, a symbolic lance, coins and for a slave, a wooden sword to indicate a grant of manumission. Those who were killed were dragged away by a figure dressed as Charon and buried outside the city or thrown into the Tiber. Many belonged to guilds who would arrange burial. An inscription in Rome records the names of 23 gladiators who belonged to a guild dedicated to Silvanus; another at Ankara records a college of retired gladiators.

Gladiators came from many ranks of society. Slaves and prisoners of war, chosen for their strength and prowess, had no choice, but others joined, some for the money, others for the love of glory or the thrill and glamour of the role. Their status was ambiguous, both despised and admired. They were an emblem of death but praised for their valour. Senators sometimes acted as gladiators in carefully arranged fights. Nero playacted as a gladiator but Commodus fought in the arena. Herodian described him as going out into the sunlight with such brilliance that it was if gold dust had been scattered before the public. He fought wild animals in the morning and often stayed in the gladiators' quarters. Both Dio Cassius and Herodian make it clear that neither wild animals nor gladiators would injure him. On one occasion he is reported to have beheaded 100 ostriches using arrows with crescent shaped heads.

Professional gladiators were trained in schools (*ludi*) by *lanistae* who would assess their qualities and allocate training schedules. The main one in Rome was the Ludus Magnus next to the Colosseum. Diet could include barley gruel with beans that gave them the name of '*hordearii*' or 'barley porridge eaters'. Galen, one of many doctors who tended to the gladiators' health and wounds, said that this could make them fat and flabby, but had one advantage – the fatty layer gave some protection against minor wounds.

Many gladiators appealed to the opposite sex, even if they were equally admired for their courage and despised for their place in society. Juvenal said that Eppia, a senator's wife, left her husband and followed a gladiator to Egypt. Faustina, Marcus Aurelius' wife, had a passion for gladiators and it was rumoured that her son Commodus was the result of a liaison with a gladiator. Gladiators could marry and inscriptions have been found in Rome recording happy marriages. One was erected to Marcus Ulpius Felix, a *murmillo*, 'her sweetest and self-deserving spouse' by his wife and Justus their son. He lived to the age of 45 but Urbicus, *secutor*, died aged 22 leaving Laurica his wife and Olympia and Fortuna, his daughters. Examination of bones in a cemetery for gladiators found at Ephesus revealed that most men died between the ages of 18 and 40.

There were some female gladiators. Petronius mentioned one brought from Britain to Rome and a possible grave of a female gladiator has been found in Britain at Southwark. One of the eight lamps placed in the grave shows a gladiator; another depicts Mercury. These women were tolerated for their novelty value. Domitian ordered them to fight at night and Martial said that he saw a fight between a female gladiator and a dwarf. Juvenal was contemptuous of these would-be Amazons:

> who has not seen one of them smiting a stump, piercing it through and through with a foil, lunging at it with a shield and going through the proper motions? Unless indeed she is nursing some further ambition in her bosom and is practising for the real arena ... What decency can a woman show wearing a helmet when she leaves her own sex behind.

Eventually Septimius Severus forbad them to appear.

THE END OF THE GAMES

Gladiatorial contests continued in spite of Constantine issuing a decree against them in AD 325, but his decision to move the capital to Constantinople led to a decline in the use of the Colosseum. In the fourth century, Valentinian I forbad Christians to be recruited as gladiators and to be sentenced to the arenas. In AD 404 there was a riot in an arena when a monk Telemachus intervened to stop a combat. When an angry crowd killed him, Honorius banned gladiatorial shows. They finally ceased in the fifth century, although animal hunts continued until AD 523. The last recorded use of the Colosseum was in AD 523 but by then much of the upper structure had gone. The demise of the games may have been the result of a shortage of volunteers and the number of slaves but there was also the considerable cost of putting on these shows. Cicero has said that if a rich man wanted to be praised, it was better that he gave a banquet or ransomed citizens from captivity.

These shows, however, had served a purpose. Juvenal summed it up: 'There was a time when the people bestowed every honour – the governance of provinces, civic leadership, military command – but now they hold themselves back; now only two things do they ardently desire – bread and circuses.' This was confirmed by Fronto, who, writing about Trajan's popularity, said that he did not neglect actors, circuses and amphitheatres knowing that the Roman people were held fast by two things above all, the grain dole and the shows, and that the success of a government depended as much on games as serious matters.

9

FOOD, DIET AND NUTRITION

The Romans are credited with having luxurious banquets with exotic food and generally gorging themselves, retiring every so often to vomit so that they could continue their indulgence. Perhaps this did happen, and Petronius's description of Trimalchio's feast probably perpetuated this stereotype, but Petronius was satirising the indulgent habits of wealthy Romans. Rome encapsulated a wide variety of eating habits, from the poor living hand to mouth to exotic banquets given by emperors for those they wished to impress.

An example of simple food is given in a poem *Moretum*, once thought to be by Virgil but now believed to be by a young poet written between 8 and 25 AD. This described the peasant Simulus rising at cockcrow to prepare his meal. He cleaned the quern, and slowly milled his flour. 'Both hands did the work, one fed in the corn, one rotated the upper stone.' Warm water mixed flour to dough. He placed dough on the hearth, put tiles over it covered with ashes. While the dough cooked, he picked four heads of garlic, parsley, rue, and coriander. He pounded these in a mortar with water, olive oil, vinegar, salt, and hard cheese to make his *moretum* eaten with bread for his midday meal. The hard work necessary to produce this simple meal was a daily task.

BASIC FOODS

Barley was used mainly for animal food. When made into bread it produced a heavy loaf and was usually regarded as food for slaves. It was also, according to Frontinus, used as a punishment. Suetonius said that Augustus disgraced a legion which had fought badly by executing every tenth man and putting the rest on an exclusive diet of barley bread. Emmer was the first main Roman wheat before being supplanted by durum wheat and bread wheat. These produced finer flour. Emmer grains, ground to provide meal for pottage and for *alica* (emmer groats), were used to make a wide variety of bread and cakes. Pliny the Elder described this as excellent food with great nutritional value.

The granaries at Ostia built in the first century AD, were enlarged under Commodus and further extended by Septimius Severus

A bakery at Pompeii. There is an oven and several mills, which would have been worked by slaves or donkeys

Roman bread varied in quality. At home it could be baked under a crock covered with hot ashes but in towns most people went to the local baker. Loaves found carbonised in Pompeii, when originally baked, would have been dense in texture and dark in colour. Columella said somewhat cynically that a bailiff when eating in the presence of slaves should eat the same bread as they did. In so doing he would make sure that the bread was carefully made. Seneca, when urging a friend to try living a poor man's life for a while said 'let your bread be hard (*durum*) and dirty (*sordidum*)'. He also said that 'Nature does not care if the bread is of coarse variety (*plebeius*) or made from the finest wheat flour (*siligneus*)'. Bread could be sprinkled with poppy seeds, baked with honey or flavoured with spices. Pliny the Elder mentioned bread made from blended wheat and bean flour and Strabo mentioned acorn bread. Grain was also used to make pottage, a staple of Roman diet especially when pieces of meat or fish were added.

Vegetables included beans, peas, onions and cabbage. Fruits included apples, apricots, cherries, figs, grapes, melons, pears, plums and quinces. Both fresh and salt water fish were sold in markets, as well as poultry, providing much needed protein, as meat was too dear for some people. Meat could be distributed during religious festivals in Rome after animals had been slaughtered as offerings to the gods. Pork was the most common meat. Varro asked, 'Who of our people cultivates a farm without keeping swine?' Sheep and goats could be eaten for their meat but were usually kept for their milk which could be made into cheese and for their hair and wool. Game was eaten in the countryside and there was no prohibition on hunting.

Essential condiments were *liquamen* and olive oil, which were produced in great quantities. *Liquamen* or *garum* – the names seem to be interchangeable – was a fermented fish sauce made by placing whole fish, preferably mackerel, in troughs and mixing them with salt. Other fish used were tunny, anchovies, sprats, even sea urchins, oysters and other shellfish. This mixture was left to ferment for anything up to three months. The reaction, which takes place when the guts of the fish react with salt to produce brine, is an enzymic proteolysis. It took place in the open; the sun hastened the process. The liquid would then be drained off ready for sale. It could be made in any quantity providing that the precise ratio of salt to fish was observed and that the product was allowed to mature for the required time. Each production area would have its own distinct taste, which might be due to the addition of wine, herbs and spices, the length of preparation time, the quantity of salt and the temperature.

Allec, the residue after the liquid was drained off, was akin to the fish paste *blachan* used in south-east Asia today. It was probably a valuable source of calcium as small bones were included. According to Pliny the Elder, *allec* was produced from a variety of fish, otherwise too small to be economically useful, and was used for a variety of purposes including cures for burns, ulcers and pains in the mouth as well as alleviating dog or crocodile bites. It could be mixed with *mulsum* until it was sweet enough to drink.

Olive tree culture was very important. Cato and Pliny the Elder gave detailed instructions about the growing and storage of olives, and the production of olive oil, as well as information of the different varieties of olives. Olive oil was used in cooking, as a marinading medium, a dressing for salads and vegetables and for conserving food. It was also used for lamp fuel, sealing wood, in perfumes, in medicine, for oiling clothes and for ritual practices. Soldiers rubbed it on their limbs in the belief that it made them supple and also oiled it onto joints in their armour. Pliny the Elder said that a happy life was one that used wine inside and olive oil outside.

Amphorae stacked at Pompeii

WINE

Vines were cultivated extensively in Italy and throughout the empire. Roman authors gave detailed instructions for planting and tending vines and the production of wine. The main production areas were Greece, Italy, Spain, Southern Gaul and North Africa. Even Britain produced some wine. From these areas it was transported to all parts of the Roman Empire although many wines were only drunk locally as they could not travel. Wine was usually drunk young although older wines are mentioned. The origins of the various wines may be discerned from the type of amphorae in which they was exported. Amphorae were often sealed internally with resin, which gave its taste to the beverage. The wine might therefore become an acquired taste or might be used medicinally as an astringent.

Winemaking was taken seriously, especially with regard to the different pressings. The first pressing was the best but the fourth produced a vinegary wine acceptable only to slaves. Writers mentioned specific wines. Pliny the Elder detailed four classes of Roman wine and listed numerous foreign ones, most of which could be tasted in Rome; Horace bemoaned the winter chill while drinking a four-year-old Sabine wine. The Romans liked spiced wine, wine sweetened with honey or even softened with gypsum or lime. *Conditum* – wine and hot water with the addition of honey pepper and spices – was a popular drink in Roman bars. Wine heated with spices was recommended as a drink for intemperance. Spiced wine could have served as a pick-me-up, a hair-of-the dog cure.

Sunken dolia in the Villa Regina, Boscoreale, Italy. When all the dolia in this area were full, it was estimated that they would have held a total of 10,000 litres (2600 gallons) of wine, which would have been allowed to age as long as was required

Wine had a great number of medicinal uses, was used as a disinfectant and to purify water. Hippocrates prescribed wine for specific illnesses and diseases. Red wine was good for digestion and white for bladder problems but wine should not be given for treating nervous diseases as it could bring on a headache. He said that it was better to be full of wine than full of food; he clearly thought it was better to be a drunkard than a glutton.

Posca, made from the poorest wines, often vinegar and mixed with herbs, was a common drink amongst poorer classes and the army. Some emperors, such as Hadrian, drank it to show they were as one with their troops. It was this drink which was offered to Christ on the cross. This was not an insult but an offering of a drink drunk by the ordinary soldier. *Must* was fresh grape juice which was often drunk in place of wine. Cato said that it had to be drunk as soon as the grapes were pressed otherwise it would ferment, but if it was boiled it became more stable. *Mulsum*, wine mixed with honey, was reputed to restore youth and potency. It was forbidden to women and slaves. *Turriculae* included sea water and fenugreek, and *carenam* was made by fermenting mature grapes with quinces. *Defrutum* was concentrated grape juice.

MEALS

Mealtimes depended on the season and varied according to individual preferences. In summer the first meal would have been taken early. Breakfast (*lenticulum*), if eaten, was as implied, breaking the night fast with a little fruit and bread, often dipped in wine. In the middle of the day a snack (*prandium*) could be vegetables, fish, cheese, eggs, meat and bread. Many Romans made this their first meal. Horace mentioned his light lunch was enough to prevent him having an empty stomach for the rest of the day.

It is likely than many families 'grazed' during the day, getting meals when they could and eating them where they wished. Children and slaves begged from the kitchen; adults might snack in the atrium or the triclinium. Not everyone wished to have a formal evening meal. When it was taken there were certain rituals that had to be observed. Patrons might entertain clients and impress them with their largess. Families could dine together and invite relatives and friends.

This meal (*cena*) could comprise three courses, some being very elaborate. A hors-d'oeuvre (*gustatio*) could be simply prepared vegetables, eggs or fish usually shellfish; oysters were especially popular. The main course (*primae mensae*) included vegetables, meats, roast or boiled, sausages or rissoles, often sharply flavoured with herbs or liquamen. Pork and poultry were the most popular meats. The Romans liked highly spiced food. In one play by the Roman poet Plautus, there was a complaint that cooks seasoned meals with condiments like screech owls, which ate the guests' intestines. The last course (*secundae mensae*) might consist of fruit, small cakes, or pastries sweetened with honey.

Wine was drunk, often in large quantities but the Romans watered their wine so that it would have a less potent effect. In wealthy households the meal could be followed by entertainments ranging from horseplay, comic actors, and jugglers to musical and literary entertainments. Pliny the Younger insisted on reading his own poems. He chided Septimius Clarus whom he had invited to dine, who would go elsewhere where he would have oysters, sows' innards, sea urchins and Spanish dancing girls. Juvenal also mentioned the delights of these girls.

Seneca knew a freedman Calvisius Sabinus who paid his slaves to memorise the works of Hesiod and Homer, but he bored the guests by repeating half forgotten lines learned from the slaves. Horace described a dinner party where the guests began with philosophical discussions, then passed to old wives' tales and ended with a guest telling the tale of the town mouse and the country mouse. Many dinners could end with hangovers and bloated stomachs.

Dinner could be served in the triclinia, which usually held three couches fitted together, set round one table. Outdoor or garden triclinia, a common feature at Pompeii, had stone couches, which could be covered with cushions. Indoor areas had wooden couches with bronze fittings, usually with a foot or headrest. In the first century BC and the first century AD, the normal arrangement was for three guests to be seated on each couch but some couches were so small that only two could have lain there.

Reclining at meals was possibly adopted in the third century BC, when Romans came into contact with the Greeks of southern Italy, although Etruscans had also exercised the custom. Livy indicated, however, that the first triclinia couches seen in Rome followed the triumph of Cn Manlius Vulso in Asia Minor in 187 BC when he brought couches, precious hangings, and specialist cooks to Rome. Boys were allowed to recline when they assumed the *toga virilis*, provided they submitted to guidance in the rules of dining. Plutarch attempted to answer a question about the possible squashing together of diners on couches. He suggested that diners lay flat on their stomachs to allow the right hand to reach for the food. When they had taken the food, they lay on their sides to give their neighbours more room.

Not all Romans agreed with the custom. Cato the Younger, on hearing of the defeat at Pharsalus, as a sign of his stoic displeasure, refused to recline except when sleeping. From then on he always sat upright at meals. In the provinces, especially the northern areas of Europe, tombstone reliefs show people sitting on stools and basket chairs eating a meal round a table.

It cannot be denied that wealthy Romans indulged themselves and this was exemplified in Petronius's satire of Trimalchio's feast in his *Satyricon*. Habinnas, one of the guests, who drunkenly arrives midway through the feast, immediately demands some wine and hot water. When asked on what he has dined, he says that the only thing missing was Trimalchio himself, 'the apple of my eye'. The feast is being given on the ninth day after a funeral of a slave, a most unusual arrangement, and Habinnas moans that he has to pour wine over the bones.

He then proceeds to describe what he has eaten. First a pig covered with sausages and served with blood puddings, beetroot and wholemeal bread. Habinnas preferred this as it was strengthening and helped his bowels. Next came cold tart and a concoction of Spanish wine poured over hot honey. This was accompanied by chickpeas, lupines, nuts and apples. He took two apples as a present for his children. He then ate over a pound of wild bear meat, as it tasted like wild boar; after all if bears could eat people why should he not eat bears? Lastly came cheese basted with new wine, snails, chitterlings, liver, eggs covered with pastry, turnips and pickled cumin seeds; bad mannered guests took three handfuls. There was ham, which the diners for some reason sent away. Habinnas, having flirted with one of Trimalchio's entertainers, ate dessert – pastry thrushes stuffed with raisins and nuts, quinces with thorns stuck in them so they resembled sea-urchins, and a curious dish looking like a fat goose surrounded by fish and all sorts of game which has been made from pork.

AMBIGUOUS DISHES

The Roman loved ambiguous dishes. Plutarch, when instructing a young man in writing poetry, wrote 'If it is true that of meats those that are not meats and of fish those that are not fish have the most flavours, let us leave the expounding of this matter to those whom Cato said that their palates are more sensitive than their mouths.' His guests would have immediately understood his meaning at a Roman dinner, where they were faced with an ambiguous dish. Hosts vied with others to surprise their guests and ordered cooks to provide dishes utilising humble ingredients, which would elicit cries of amazements when the dish was presented. Horace mentioned a Trojan pig, so called because it was full of other creatures like the Trojan Horse was full of men.

Trimalchio remarked that his chef could produce any food made from another – a fish out of a sow's belly, a pigeon out of lard and a turtledove out of ham. Petronius was stressing one of the features of a banquet, which the Romans loved – the surprise items, either disguised foods or the unexpected happening. Apicius's cookery book provided recipes of *patinae* (pâtes) where authentic ingredients created something completely different. Three recipes are headed 'Salt fish without fish', which used hare, kid, lamb or chicken liver, moulded into a fish-like shape, sprinkled with oil and mixed with herbs, liquamen and ground walnuts. Another, 'a patina of anchovy without anchovies' utilises the authentic ingredients of boiled fish mixed with pepper, rue, liquamen and eggs, together with jellyfish, 'taking care by cooking in steam that these do not mix with the eggs'. This recipe confidently stated, 'at table no one will know what he is eating.'

Surprise dishes were popular. Trimalchio's cook was a past master at this. A huge bearded fellow, presumably the cook, brought in a dish on which was a wild boar. He cut it open and out flew a flock of thrushes. Fowlers with nets caught them so that the birds could be used again for this trick or be prepared for table. To carry the joke further, Trimalchio asked the guests to look at the delicious acorns on which the boar had been fed. The guests recoiled when these 'acorns' were handed out but they were two kinds of juicy dates. A similar trick was played later when the boar, seemingly cooked, appeared again. Trimalchio 'looked closer and closer' at it, complained that it not been gutted, and ordered the cook to be whipped. The cook pleaded for mercy, gutted the pig and out poured sausages and blood puddings.

A surprise could be at the expense of the lower classes. Juvenal described the difference in the food which Virro ate and that offered to a poor client. This included vintage wines and fine bread against course wine and pieces of hard, mouldy bread.

> Look at the lobster which is brought to the master. It is carried on a dish walled with asparagus as high as a tall attendant ... [the client is] served with a crayfish, hemmed in by an egg cut in half; a funeral supper upon on a tiny plate.

COOKS AND COOKERY BOOKS

Cooks might be slaves attached to the household or they could be professionals hired for some occasion, often chosen from a group which hung about in a market place. When hired, they

Pans on the stove of the House of the Vettii, Pompeii

tried to assume dominance over any domestic slaves in a household because they regarded themselves as professionals. Nevertheless even though they might despise the household slaves they had to keep on good terms with them because the slaves knew the routine of the household, the master's preferences and, on a basic level, where cooking implements were kept. A wary tolerance resulted. Hired cooks had the right to keep any food that was not used and sell it for their own profit. When accused of pilfering, Plautus' cook remarked in amicable tones 'Can it be that you expect us to find a cook without a kite's or eagle's claws'. It is perhaps not surprising that their patron goddess was Laverna, goddess of thieves.

According to Livy many had made a first appearance in Rome in 189 BC, the specific date relating to cooks brought to Rome as booty after Gnaeus Manlius Vulso's campaign in Galatia. Before that they had been 'the most worthless of slaves'. Later they became a profession and formed guilds. One guild is mentioned on an inscription found at Praeneste dedicated to the goddess Fortuna Primigenia.

Cooks knew their worth and if they were freedmen could earn a wage and set their own standards. Martial grumbled that a cook must not have the palate of a slave – he ought to possess the taste of his master. Both he and Livy implied that cooks were becoming more pretentious and that cookery had become an art form, but Seneca satirised a man whom he called a 'professor of the science of the cook shop' and excluded cooks from the liberal arts, which were pursued by intellectuals. Cicero also displayed his contempt for cooks. He placed cookery amongst the sordid food trades, which cater for sensual pleasures and thus not a profession becoming to a gentleman.

The Romans had several cookery books of which the most well known is that of Apicius; however, there are three potential authors of that name. The first Apicius lived in the late

first century BC, being mentioned by Poseidonius for his love of luxury. The second, M. Gavius Apicius, was a renowned gourmet living during the reign of Tiberius. When hearing there were large shrimps to be found in Libya, he sailed there, tasted them and completely unimpressed, sailed back to Italy without bothering to go ashore. He is best known for his manner of death. He spent 60 million sesterces on food and feasting. According to Seneca, on finding that he had only 10 million sesterces left, he drank poison, 'You never did anything, Apicius, more gluttonous'. The third Apicius, according to Athenaeus, lived during Trajan's reign and is best known for his advice on transporting oysters.

The work bearing the name of Apicius is a collection of recipes apparently compiled in the fourth or early fifth century from the second-century Apicius's books, together with snippets from elsewhere, such as a book of household hints by Apuleius, some of whose work has survived in the *Geoponica,* and certain medical writings from Marcellus, a physician living at the time of Nero.

Fragments of other cookery books have survived, some in references by classical writers. Cato, Varro and Columella, who were principally concerned with farming methods and agriculture, left some recipes. Dietary writers such as Anthimus and authors of medical textbooks such as Galen and Orsibasius also included recipes. Few recipes, even those of Apicius, note any quantities or measurement. This is to be expected as good cooks rely on their own experience when cooking and rarely measure out ingredients precisely. Cato is perhaps unusual in that he does give quantities, as for example in his cake recipes.

EPULUM AND CONVIVIUM

The term *epulum,* the name given to a Roman feast, was first a meal associated with some religious function such as the *Ludi Romani.* In time its religious connotation diminished, and the term was associated with opulent feasts provided for the public. The *convivium* in its simplest form was a meal for friends and was intended both to express a relationship between equals as well as being an opportunity for patrons to entertain clients and probably show off their wealth. In time *epulum* and *convivium* both came to mean large public feasts in a variety of contexts, for feeding and entertaining many more people than just the friends of the host.

Women sometimes participated in the *convivium.* In 7 BC Livia, the wife of Augustus entertained the wives of senators while her son Tiberius entertained the senators at a dinner in the portico of Livia. She had wanted to entertain both together, but Tiberius insisted on the separation of the sexes.

In the first century BC Lucullus's extravagance became notorious. Once when Caesar and Pompey were invited to dine with him they agreed but said they would dine with him that day, hoping that he would be unable to let his servants know and thereby would be forced to provide a simple meal. Lucullus outwitted them, for he told his servants he would dine with his guests 'in Apollo'. Each dining room had fixed allowances for dinners and Apollo served the most costly.

Public banquets, often on a lavish scale, were held by magistrates before elections and by family members to mark deaths or celebrate birthdays. Generals feasted their troops after

Reconstruction of a Roman kitchen, Fishbourne Roman Villa, England

battles, senators fed their clients, and decurions and aediles entertained fellow citizens or their peers. Distinguished citizens provided banquets for the populace, often to gain the favours of the crowd. By partaking in a banquet one acknowledged the superiority of the provider.

To celebrate his triumph over Mithridates and Tigranes in 62 BC Lucullus is said to have given a banquet for the senate and provided sacrificial feasts for the people, which included 1 million jars of Greek wine, probably equivalent to 4 million litres. Crassus in 70 BC feasted 10,000 tables of people after a sacrifice to Hercules and gave each person an additional allowance of grain for three months. In 45 BC Julius Caesar gave a feast with 22,000 dining couches. Allowing three people to a couch this would mean 66,000 people were feasted. Such generosity was not confined to the elite. An inscription at Ostia records that P. Lucilius Gamala gave a feast on 217 dining couches and on two occasions provided a lunch (*prandium*) for the *coloni*.

Emperors sought to gain favour by providing public banquets in addition to private dinners. Claudius entertained hundreds of guests and even went so far as to pass an edict allowing flatulence at banquets after he learned that one of his guests was acutely uncomfortable through modesty. One of the most memorable entertainments was that given in the Colosseum by Domitian in AD 84. Slaves handed out white napkins to the crowd. Fruits included luxurious ones from the east – plums from Damascus, dates from Pontus and Palestine, figs from Asia Minor and apples and pears from Armorica. Pastries distributed included some in the shape of human figures. Roasted flamingos, pheasants and guinea fowl were tossed into the crowd for people to take home. Wine flowed freely, and the crowd was entertained by troops of dancing Lydian ladies, troops of Syrians and by gladiatorial fights, including several between pygmies.

Dio Cassius recorded a banquet given by Domitian to his senators in a room draped with black, with couches and tables covered with black clothes. By each guest was a tombstone recorded with his name. Naked boys painted black served the guests and the food provided was that which was usually offered to the dead. The senators kept silent while Domitian commented on death and slaughter. When the guests left they found unknown slaves waiting to escort them. When they arrived home in great relief there was immediately a knock on the door. Expecting a summons for execution they were relieved to find that the messengers brought costly dishes from the feast and tombstones that turned out to be made of silver.

Suetonius recorded Nero's decree that every day his officials should hand out 1000 birds of every kind, food parcels, tokens for corn, clothing, gold, silver, farm beasts, wild animals and even agricultural lands. Seemingly it was potluck what was received. Wealthy patrons distributed bread, pastries and sweet wine to the populace to celebrate their election to office or when a building was dedicated.

Collegia held feasts partly to maintain the solidarity between members and partly because some collegia were composed of slaves or freedmen who had no family ties. Varro complained that 'such dinners are now so countless that they make the price of provisions go soaring.' Collegia buildings have been identified at Pompeii and Ostia. One building at Ostia founded during the reign of Hadrian seems to have been the collegia of the carpenters (*fabri tignuarii*). A central court, surrounded by rooms, is extended by a wing containing four triclinia with masonry couches, indicating that dining was one of the main functions of the collegium.

Inscriptions on reliefs indicate the munificence of the feasts provided. In Gabii decurions and members of the priestly college of the *seviri Augustales* banqueted in public on separate triclinia. M. Cacius Cerna, who lived at Sinuessa in the Campania after a distinguished political and military career, founded a public feast for the people of his locality to be held each year on his birthday. Cocceia Vera from Cura allocated money for a public feast to be held on her birthday with the guests arranged strictly in order of status. Decurions were placed on 10 triclinia, *seviri* being seated on two or more and so on thus reflecting the social spectrum. In Corfinium, a donor left a legacy endowing a fund with the interest providing a feast to remember him on the anniversary of his birthday.

Plebeians loved these feasts. Valerius Maximus said that 'For while people approved of private frugality, publicly they set more store by a handsome show'. Seneca qualified this implying that the Roman people loathed luxury but they loved public splendour. 'They do not like extravagant banquets but much less do they like shabbiness or meanness'. Cicero says that Cato the Elder disapproved of feasts, indicating that it was wrong to promote goodwill by providing food. He added that some feasts went badly awry. Quintus Aelius Tubero was asked by his cousin Quintus Fabius Maximus to organize a funerary banquet for the people of Rome on the death of his uncle, Scipio Aemilianus. Tubero, however, was a stoic and therefore covered the couches with shabby goatskins and provided poor samian ware, which was declared by the people to be more appropriate for the death of Diogenes the Cynic than to honour the death of the mighty Africanus. In consequence the people voted against Tubero when he stood for praetor in the next election.

Feasts also had to be provided for unexpected guests. In 45 BC Cicero wrote to Atticus that Julius Caesar stayed with him overnight. Unfortunately this included all his retinue, who had to be entertained in three dining rooms, and 2000 soldiers, although Cicero probably did not have to feed them. Caesar had a bath, oiled his body and came into dinner. As he was 'following

a course of emetics', he was able to partake of 'a fine well appointed meal' and he indicated that he had dined well. Cicero provided his guests with all they had wanted and boasted that 'I showed that I knew how to live'. He added wryly that

> they were not the kind of persons to whom one says, 'Do come again when you are next in the neighbourhood'. Once is enough. It was a visit or should I call it a billeting, which was troublesome to me but not disagreeable.

DRINKING AND EATING ESTABLISHMENTS

There were numerous bars and taverns in Rome, together with street vendors who sold hot or cold food and provided what could be considered as cheap, low-grade fast food. Their cries, according to Seneca disturbed honest people in their houses. Bars, taverns and inns were also to be found in other towns and many have been identified in Ostia, Pompeii and Herculaneum. These provided meeting places for the various social classes to mingle and were essential social bases for the urban poor. Magistrates might be suspicious because they attracted young men from the patrician class who sought adventure by plotting against the Senate.

The emperors tried to control them. Tiberius restricted the amount of food sold in fast food establishments, even banning bread and cakes. Nero restricted food sold in taverns to green vegetables and dried beans, yet he spent a great deal of his time in taverns dressed as a slave. Vespasian even forbad anything to be sold in taverns except pulses. It is uncertain, however, how far these regulations could be or were enforced.

The attractions of these establishments included gambling; many undoubtedly were brothels, as inscriptions outside some of the Pompeian establishments make clear. One bar had a painting showing gambling and one man boasted as he scrawled on the wall that he had 'won 855 sesterii at Nuceria without cheating'. Juvenal sneered at the consul Lateranus for frequenting all-night taverns, where a shameless barmaid lies in wait when he should be preparing to defend the borders of the empire upon the Rhine or the Danube.

A *taberna* could refer to both a shop and a bar, usually a single room with a masonry counter encased within which were large dolia for dry foods – grains, legumes, chickpeas, fruit and nuts. Wine was kept in amphorae placed horizontally on a rack. The kitchen was at the back and there might be a latrine. Taverns were placed on street corners to attract trade, as many pubs in England are today. Scenes at Pompeii show diners seated and standing while drinking, and men playing dice. Bars hang from the ceiling holding hams, sausages, vegetables and other food. Sidonius Apollinaris, a fifth-century AD Latin poet, who in AD 486 became Bishop of Clermont, mentioned taking refuge in a dingy tavern in Gaul where the smoke from the kitchen made him choke. With eyes watering he saw steam from cooking pots mingling with the smoke from hot frying pans, where sausages were sizzling, flavoured with thyme and juniper berries.

A *thermopolium* was a bar where quick snacks and drinks were served. Many of these were found lining the streets of Pompeii. A *popina* was a drinking and eating establishment with a somewhat dubious reputation as the haunt of thieves, drunks and prostitutes. An *uncta popina* is what in Britain might be called a greasy spoon café and *immundae popinae* (foul bars) probably refers to the smoky atmosphere caused by the brazier used for heating as well as smells

Funerary relief of a wineshop.
(Musée Archéologique de Dijon)

Graffiti from Pompeii, probably
from outside an inn, displaying
the fare within,' which included
pig's head and something which
looks like a kebab

from cooking and stale food. In Pompeii many *popinae* were next to bathing establishments so that customers could get snacks and return to their daily routine without wasting time. Juvenal mentioned a chain-gang ditcher nostalgic for the smell of tripe in some hot crowded cook shop.

A *caupona* referred to an inn where travellers could stay the night in shared rooms or even shared beds, but it was also a place which sold drinks and fast food. They sometimes provided stabling for mules and horses. Extras were available in the form of dancing girls and prostitutes. Cicero in his speech *Against Piso* described his opponent leaving lunch in a *caupona* with a hood pulled over his head and his breath reeking with fumes from eating in a stinking bar. Innkeepers put up a menu giving the price of food and drink and a night's lodging. One at Pompeii showed a painted menu – chicken, fish, ham and peacock.

One innkeeper at the 'Inn of Euxinus' near the amphitheatre at Pompeii had a small vineyard by its side to supply his own wine to customers. These could drink at the small bar at the main entrance or in more relaxed fashion in a large open area to the rear. Two large *dolia* found on the site each had a capacity of 454 litres (100 gallons). This was more than a small vineyard would produce but the owner probably also bought wine from elsewhere. Wine amphorae found on the site were labelled with the innkeeper's address: *Pompeis ad amphitheatr Euxino caponi.*

DIET AND NUTRITION

Food is a necessity and often quantity not quality was the criterion for Romans. Supply depended on the season and on distribution. The aim was self-sufficiency but famines and shortages could make for uneven distribution. Surplus products were bartered or sold in markets. Poorer people were worst off. Examination of teeth of many adults found in 1980 in the boat shelters at Herculaneum in which they had taken refuge showed enamel hypoplasia (stress marks), which indicated periods of arrested growth due to poor nutrition. At Pompeii teeth revealed rings in the enamel, which indicated periods of infectious disease during childhood. Obviously some Romans ate better than others and they might have suffered for this. Over indulgence of food and wine would have sometimes resulted in liver complaints, heart attacks and obesity. A rich diet, especially if laced with *liquamen*, caused bad breath.

Roman adult taste tended towards the spicy and the robust. The Romans disliked blandness and added contrived sour, spicy and bitter tastes by using herbs and spices. They countered those flavours by adding *liquamen* or olive oil. The oil blunted the bitter phytonutrients and, unknown to the Romans, had the added advantage of containing vitamin E.

Seneca was contemptuous of Roman gluttony:

> from every quarter the Romans gather together every known and unknown thing to tickle a fastidious palate; the food which their stomachs by weakened indulgence can scarcely retain is fetched from the farthest oceans. They vomit that they might eat; they eat that they may vomit. They do not deign even to digest the feasts for which they ransack the whole earth.

Persius contemptuously mentioned a person who ignored the advice of his doctor:

Edible fish portrayed on a mosaic possibly from Populonia near Naples. In the centre is a lobster. Clockwise from right: dentex, gilt-headed bream, red mullet, comber, common bass, green wrasse, scorpion fish, moray eel, octopus. (British Museum)

Bloated with food and queasy of stomach he goes to bathe with sulphurous belching issuing from his throat. But as he drinks his wine a shivering fit comes over him and knocks the hot glass from his hands; his bared teeth chatter, the savoury morsels drop from his slack lips. Then follow the trumpet and the candles and last the dear deceased, laid out on a high bier, and smeared with greasy unguents, sticks out his stiff heels towards the door.

Yet it is possible that most Romans followed what is now considered to be the laudable Mediterranean diet, comprising mainly pulses, cereals, vegetables, fruits, olive oil, cheese, fish and only a little meat. Obviously this depended on availability. Fish is rich in lysine and amino acids, and a good source of protein; calcium is gained from eating bones and fluorine helps to prevent tooth decay. People living near the coast or a river would eat fish, and the Romans developed fish farming and provided supplies of salted fish. Fish needs to be sold and consumed rapidly. Growth of bacteria means that it deteriorates quickly, becoming dangerous to health. Pliny the Elder and Columella warned against eating fish that was not fresh. Iron is found in molluscs so the huge consumption of oysters would have been beneficial. The Romans imported them from all over the empire. Juvenal commented on large numbers coming from Britain, probably transported in barrels with constantly renewed seawater. Some of the best were Brundisian oysters fattened in Lake Lucrine in the Bay of Naples. Oysters were considered to be an aphrodisiac, hence their popularity.

Beef, pork, mutton and lamb provide protein, but cereals and pulses were dominant foods in the ancient world, especially for the poor, soldiers and urban residents. One problem with a mainly cereal diet and especially bread made with a high fibre content is that although it protected the teeth from decay because it was abrasive and scoured the teeth more than

did a highly refined diet, if the flour was not sieved well the grit remained in the baked loaf, which wore down teeth, making them increasingly sensitive, especially if the pulp inside a tooth was reached.

Lucretius said that teeth had a share in the sensations of the body, as was shown by toothache and the twinge of cold water and biting on a sharp stone in a piece of bread. Oral hygiene was a problem, as was toothache. Celsus said that 'toothache was the greatest of torments.' Pliny the Elder suggested henbane to alleviate it. Teeth from Pompeii reveal evidence of the build up of calculus, which was picked off by the many toothpicks found. Martial recommended using a quill. Pliny advised that teeth should be cleaned with the toothpick and a mixture of ground up oyster shells and charcoal. As this was unpleasant, it was mixed with honey, which would of course have undone any good work. Even so, many Romans probably inflicted their friends and neighbours with bad breath.

A cereal diet also contains phytate acid; the consumption of this component interferes with the absorption of calcium and iron thus predisposing individuals to rickets and osteomalacia. These have been found in skeletons in Roman cemeteries indicating a lack of vitamin D. Vitamin

Relief of an oculist treating a patient

D helps the body to absorb calcium and can be obtained from egg yolks, liver and fish oils. The best source is the action of sun on the skin, which would have been normal in the climate of Italy. Children of the upper classes in Rome, however, were swaddled and kept indoors rather than allowed to run free, which would have created a propensity towards rickets. Children of the poorer classes would have had more freedom but an early life of hard labour helping their parents could cause other problems.

The Romans did not seem to have drunk much milk, possibly because of a problem with lacto-intolerance, but they had many varieties of cheese and this would have helped their calcium intake. A lack of liver, kidneys and fish oils could result in eye diseases such as night-blindness and keratomalacia, a softened, perforated cornea. Galen recorded over 100 eye problems. Celsus and Hippocrates gave details of eye operations including the removal of cataracts, and needles for this operation have been found on sites far distant from Rome. Eye surgeons and eye operations are commemorated on tombstones. Roman oculists' stamps with carved retrograde inscriptions, pressed into cakes of eye salve, indicate that their recipients hoped for a cure.

Obviously not everyone suffered from disease or malnutrition. The Romans introduced new crops to different parts of the empire and some plants were improved through crossbreeding with native ones, yielding hardier and more productive foodstuffs. Selective breeding produced larger sheep and cattle. If people knew nothing of nutrition, they knew what plants made them feel well and those they felt were harmful to them. It can be assumed that many Romans ingested a reasonable balance of protein, vitamins, minerals and calories, providing that sufficient food was available.

Some skeletons in Romano-British cemeteries and at Herculaneum have a high bone-lead content. In the short term this could have been caused in a soft water area by the drinking water running in lead pipes, but it also reflected a lifetime accumulation. Some children died of lead poisoning, possibly due to transfer from their mothers' milk. Those who survived into middle age ingested it from food cooked or resting in lead pans or through fruit juices and wine prepared in lead or pewter vessels. The acidity of the fruit caused traces of lead to dissolve, and fruit juices were sometimes added to wine so that the amount of lead intensified in the solution. Persons suffering from lead poisoning developed a metallic taste in the mouth, experienced lack of appetite, digestive trouble and diarrhoea. To counter the lack of appetite sufferers would eat more highly spiced and seasoned food, common in Roman cookery.

Inhumations at Selinunte in Sicily showed that Roman adults and children had furrows in their eye sockets indicating a lack of iron, possibly due to food shortages. Some of the skeletons at Herculaneum had high zinc readings, which can be attributed to a high consumption of crustaceans, oysters, dry fruit and legumes. This diet, which lacks meat protein, would also have caused anaemia.

There were other health problems in the Roman world, but their existence has to be partly inferred. Pliny the Elder noted that 'diseases attack not only entire nations but also particular classes, sometimes slaves, sometimes nobility and likewise other grades.' Hepatitis would have been common, as would bacteria producing salmonella. The comparatively low standards of sanitation, people depositing excrement and carcasses of dead animals in the street and the general filth would have resulted in disease spreading quickly, especially those spread by faecal-oral transmission. These included gastroenteritis, parasitic worms such as threadworms, roundworms and whipworms, and diarrhoea.

Roman bathing establishments helped to ensure that the majority of the citizens were relatively clean but equally the warm waters provided a breeding ground for bacteria, especially as some physicians recommended patients to use the baths to help with skin diseases and other ailments. Much of southern Italy was covered with swamps with malaria-carrying mosquitoes; Columella warned against houses being built near marshes from which came mysterious diseases. Malaria is likely to have killed Augustus. It was not until Mussolini drained the Pontine Marshes in the 1920s that malaria was finally eliminated in southern Italy.

Natural and manmade disasters included hurricanes (Campania AD 66), earthquakes (Antioch AD 115), volcanic eruptions (Vesuvius AD 79) and fires (Rome AD 64). Tacitus mentioned the collapse of an amphitheatre (Fidenae AD 27). There were deaths and injuries from war, piracy and brigands. Plague took an enormous toll. Cassius Dio mentioned 2000 people a day dying from plague in Rome in AD 189 and Suetonius said 30,000 died during Nero's reign; Tacitus said that no one was spared. Famines were frequent not only because of failure of crops but also as a consequence of war and the difficulty of transporting food.

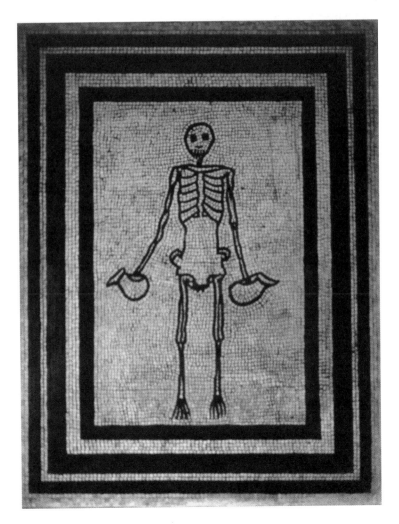

Mosaic of a skeleton in the Museo Archeologico Nazionale, Naples. This type of mosaic was popular, representing the brevity of life with the two jugs indicating 'drink up and be merry'

LIFE EXPECTANCY

Estimates of the average life expectancy in Rome vary between 20 to 30 years from birth. This seems to contradict the reported ages at which men achieved public office as previously stated. Further evidence is required to reconcile these figures. There were numerous deaths in infancy and early childhood, bringing down the average. In Rome itself the average age of death for men has been calculated at 22, for women 19 but in other parts of the empire it could be higher. In Spain it was calculated to be 37 for men and 34 for women. Female life expectancy was lower because of the dangers of childbirth and puerperal fever. In Africa the average seems to have been higher. Sallust, in his account of the war with Jugurtha, commented 'the natives are healthy, swift of foot and great endurance. They commonly die of old age unless they fall to the steel or wild beasts for disease seldom gets the better of them, but the country abounds in wild animals.' Tax census data from Egypt also indicates that life expectancy could be greater than that at Rome.

Keith Hopkins, in his analysis of the age of death mentioned on tombstones, suggested that tombstones indicate not only the mortality of the commemorated but also of the survival of the commemorated. Because of the different ages of the sexes at marriage, wives might be expected to commemorate their husbands; a wife might be commemorated only if her husband survived her. Husbands were on an average nine years older than wives and might be expected to predecease them. Hopkins argued that life expectancy was fewer than 30, and deaths from infant mortality averaged about 200 in 1000. This allows for replacement of the population but not for a huge increase.

Some people lived to a great age. Pliny the Elder quoted from the census figures of certain areas in Italy when both men and women were living to an age of over 100. A tombstone from Caerleon mentions Julius Valens who died aged 100; another mentions his wife Julia Secundina who died aged 75. Pusa, son of Trougillius died aged 120 at Mainz, but how far these ages are accurate is uncertain.

Evidence from tombstones also commemorates only the elite. Evidence from bones in cemeteries may be more accurate. The cemetery at Lankhills in Winchester contained 284 skeletons, 64 of which died in their early twenties and only 52 survived beyond the age of 36. At the Trentholme Drive cemetery in York, out of 231 males the age at death varies from 25 to 50 but this might be because York was a legionary fortress and soldiers were better fed than civilians. At the Graeco-Roman cemetery at Gabbari in Alexandria out of 55 skeletons at least two-thirds had died under the age of 20.

Probably Pliny the Elder spoke truly when he said that 'Whatever this gift of nature bestowed on us, it is uncertain and insecure, indeed sinister and of brief duration, even in the case of those to whose lot it has fallen in most bounteous measure, at all events when we regard the whole extent of time.'

10

TRAVEL AND TRANSPORT

ROADS

The Romans have always been admired for their excellent system of roads, which they constructed throughout the empire. Roads could form a boundary or a frontier. They could control the population by enabling the army to march swiftly to put down rebellions, but basically they provided for the movement of traffic – slow lumbering carts taking goods to market, messengers on horseback carrying dispatches for the administration and marching soldiers making their way from camp to camp. Not every road was the same. Tracks used by pedestrians and pack animals could be gravel and dirt paths, often with steep gradients and tight bends. For more frequented ways Roman engineering techniques provided a highly efficient surface maintained by local communities or landowners whose land bordered them. The army especially in frontier provinces constructed some roads. The Romans had probably learned the technique of making substantial roads from the Etruscans. In Italy roads were managed by *curatores viarum* and Augustus put these on an official footing, either managing one road or several roads.

Although roads had often been constructed in response to military needs they were available to everyone free of tolls. Strabo said that the Romans had more foresight than the Greeks in providing roads, aqueducts and sewers. The Romans knew the worth of these roads often commemorating their opening by the building of an arch such as that erected at Beneventum in Trajan's honour to celebrate the extension of the Appian Way. An inscription on the base of the statue of Appius Claudius in the Forum of Augustus noted that when he was Censor (312 BC) he had begun the construction of this road and Diodorus Siculus understood this when he commented that although with this road of more than 1000 *stadii* (about 185km; 115 miles) he had spent the entire revenues of the state, Appius had left a deathless monument.

So great was the achievement of road building that emperors and families were proud to give their names to roads – the Aurelii, the Valerii, the Aemilii. Statius, in one of his poems, praised the building of the Via Domitiana, a branch of the Appian Way to Naples.

Arch of Trajan at Beneventum (Benevento) erected c.AD 114 to commemorate the completion of the Via Traiana

He rejoiced in the improvement of the road from 'one where the unkindly earth sucked in the wheels of a vehicle to one where a journey can be made in two hours rather than the whole day.'

CONSTRUCTION

Procopius, in his *History of the Gothic Wars* written in the late fifth century, describing Belisarius's advance on Rome commented on the survival over 900 years of the Appian Way, which he called 'the Queen of Roads'. The broad width of the road allowed wagons going in opposite directions to pass easily.

Basalt block paving in a street at Pompeii

Appius had:

worked the stones until they were smooth and flat and, cutting them into a polygonal shape, he fastened them together without putting concrete or anything between them, and they were fastened together so securely and the joints were so firmly closed, that they give the appearance of having grown together. And after the passage of time and after being traversed by many wagons and all kinds of animals every day, they have neither separated at all at the joints, nor has any of the stones been worn out or reduced in thickness – indeed they have not lost any of their polish.

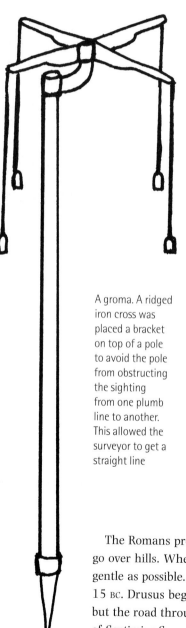

A groma. A ridged iron cross was placed a bracket on top of a pole to avoid the pole from obstructing the sighting from one plumb line to another. This allowed the surveyor to get a straight line

Silius's poetic description of the construction of a road said that it was first necessary to prepare furrows to mark out the boundaries of a road, then to hollow out the ground. A base must be made for 'the road's arched rise' lest the soil give way and a 'niggardly bottom provides a treacherous bed for the packed stones.' After that the road should have even blocks set close together and held with wedges. Gangs of men would cut down forests or divert streams; some trimmed beams and boulders, others 'bind stones together, interlacing the work with baked sand and dirty tufa.'

This is basically correct. Land surveyors (*agrimensores*), organised and trained under the empire, carefully measured and laid out roads using a *groma* and a *chorobate*. By aligning the lines the surveyors could survey right angles and straight lines. Roads were usually between 2.3m (8ft) to 4.73m (16ft) wide. This allowed wagons to pass or overtake. The best roads had four layers. The lowest was a layer of stones placed on a mortar bed. Next more stones mixed with mortar were added. These two layers provided a firm foundation. A third layer contained even more mortar. The top layer could be of cut stones or gravel. When the road was repaired with another layer the road was often arched above the surface of the surrounding ground and drainage channels on either side allowed the water to run off. Sometimes pavements of beaten earth or crushed gravel were provided.

The Romans preferred to construct roads on flat ground rather than go over hills. When they were forced to do this gradients were kept as gentle as possible. They began to construct roads across the Alps about 15 BC. Drusus began the Via Claudia Augusta from Trent to Augsburg but the road through the Brenner Pass was not finished until the reign of Septimius Severus. Such roads were always travelled with care. Strabo gave a graphic description of dangers encountered: masses of rock and

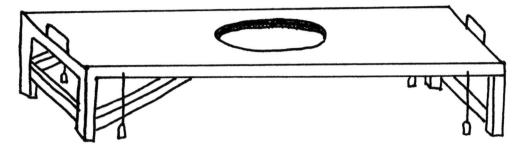

A chorobate. The tabletop had a tray of water set into it, which acted as a spirit level. The table was set on the ground and sightings were taken through two iron hoops at each end of the table. When the ground sloped stones could be placed under the legs of one end of the table.

enormous frowning cliffs, which sometimes fell away beneath the road so that 'if one made the slightest mishap the peril was such that there was no escape since the fall was to chasms abysmal.' To prevent cliff falls, retaining walls were built. Nothing deterred Roman road builders. Marshy ground was crossed by logs and withies as Tacitus mentioned in his history of Germanicus's campaign against the Germans in AD 15. Near Rochester in Britain piles were driven into the ground; in Belgium piling was replaced by weaves of horizontal and vertical wattle.

The army or local gangs provided the labour. Making roads was one way of keeping the army busy in the provinces. Livy said that the consul, Flaminius, in order not to allow soldiers to become idle made them construct a road between Arezzo and Bologna. During Tiberius's reign troops constructing a road in Noricum rebelled and forced their officers to work with them.

MILESTONES

Roads were provided with milestones, which marked each Roman mile and recorded the distance from the start of the road or from the last city passed through. Plutarch credited Gaius Gracchus with promoting the numbering of miles on little stone columns in a *Lex Viaria* in 123 BC. Miles were measured by means of a *hodometer* fixed to a cart, which had special wheels, 1.2m (4 Roman feet) in diameter and 3.7m (12.5 Roman feet) in circumference. 400 revelations made one Roman mile at which point a pebble was dropped into a metal bowl. Gracchus also provided mounting blocks at smaller intervals so that equestrians could mount their horses without assistance. In 20 BC Augustus erected the *Miliarium Aureum* (Golden Milestone), a marble column covered with gilt bronze in the Forum with the distances to the great cities of the empire written on it. Pliny the Younger wrote to his friend Gallus that to visit his Laurentian villa, which was about 17 miles from Rome, he could take two routes. He could leave either at the fourteenth milestone or at the eleventh. Whichever one he took these roads were very sandy, suitable for a man of horseback but not good for heavy loads. Compensation was provided by the splendid views on either side.

Remains of the Miliarium Aureum, Forum Romanum. In antiquity this was a marble column covered with gilt bronze recording the distances to the great cities of the empire. Only a fragment of the shaft and a base with some marble decoration remain

Milestones, usually 3m (9ft) high and placed about 3m (9ft) from the edge of the road surface, recorded the distance in miles or *pedes*. 1000 *pedes* was equivalent to 1478m (1617yds). Milestones often recorded the name of the official who had ordered the construction of the road, those who had improved it, and even the method of construction and repair. One milestone on the Via Appia records Hadrian's restoration work and indicates that the expense was to be shared between the emperor and local landowners. Another boasted that Caracalla spent his own money in repairing the road with new flint stones that would be better for travellers.

BRIDGES

The Romans preferred where possible to ford a river as this was cheap and easy to maintain when provided with a stone base, but sometimes bridges were necessary. Sometimes they were of a single arched span and later widened, as was the Ponte di Nona on the Via Praenestina, which had a remarkable seven spans. Usually bridges had three arches; the central one was flattened, the two outer ones were curved with the roads leading up onto the bridge as flattened as possible. In northern Europe wooden bridges were built either with wooden piles or stone pillars. When Caesar wished to cross the Rhine he considered it beneath his dignity to cross by boat. He therefore ordered a bridge to be built which was done with great difficulty on account of the swiftness, width and depth of the river. He boasted that the bridge was constructed in 10 days with no problem for the men.

Model of Caesar's bridge. (Rheinisches Museum, Bonn)

TUNNELS

Occasionally tunnels had to be constructed, both for water supply and for road passage. The first tunnels were reputed to have been built near Naples by Lucius Cocceius Auctus in the late first century BC near Cumae. One tunnel has a length of 7km (4.3 miles) and the Cripta Neapolitana between Pozzuoli and Naples has a length of 705m (771 yds). Seneca, in a letter to a friend, mentions this being dimly lit by torches and extremely dusty and muddy. Other tunnels include that made on the Via Flaminia on the Furlo Pass in the first century AD.

CITY STREETS

In Rome most of the city streets were narrow, the widest being about 2.44m (8ft). Even after the fire in AD 64 attempts to widen the street were frustrated because of the high price of land and the fact that citizens wanted to restart heir businesses quickly. Pompeii had both wide and narrow streets; the Via di Mercurio is 9.25m (32ft) wide and the Via Dell' Abondanza 8.53m (28ft) wide. Side streets vary between 1.83m and 2.44m (6 and 8ft). Presumably those with pavements did not allow vehicles to pass easily and there may have been a one-way system. Planned towns, such as the colonia for veterans established in other parts of the empire, had ample street widths. Those at Colchester were 17–20ft (5–6m); at Xanten they were 10–12m (33–40ft). Both were modelled on the chessboard fashion of the Roman forts.

The city streets were maintained by aediles; usually their authority ended at the city gates but it could be extended to 10 miles beyond. They could order householders or tenants to keep the streets clear of rubbish in front of their dwellings and how far this happened would depend on their forceful nature. Public filth carts trundled round to collect rubbish and animal and human excrement. Seneca complained bitterly about filthy streets, dirty people and tenement walls cracked and crumbling. Juvenal said that the streets were full of obstacles and moaned that crowds crushed him, that his legs were caked with mud, and that the continual traffic in the narrow streets caused problems. He suggested that people should make a will before going out to dinner in case domestic waste, a vase, broken pottery or the contents of a chamber pot thrown out of an upper window hit them. Pavements, as can still be seen at Pompeii, were often raised above street level. There were stepping-stones at intervals to allow people to cross the street and these would also have slowed traffic.

In 45 BC Julius Caesar tried to prohibit circulation of carts and carriages in Rome from sunrise to the tenth hour (about 3pm in the afternoon) except for those transporting construction materials for temples, public works and to take away demolition material. Vestal Virgins and priests were allowed to ride in chariots. This meant that traffic trundled through the streets all night. Juvenal moaned that people died of insomnia; 'Only if you have a lot of money can you sleep in Rome.' Martial echoed him: 'When I wish to sleep, I go to my villa.' There were no traffic regulations. British archaeologists, studying wheel ruts in a limestone quarry at Blackstone Edge, Swindon, have suggested that carts drove on the left, but it is uncertain if this applied throughout the empire. Drivers probably fought for space on the streets. Slaves of wealthy people would make sure that their masters had right of way.

The Via dell' Abondanza, Pompeii, was one of the main arteries of the city. Part of it was closed to prevent wheeled vehicles entering the Forum

The Cardo Maxima, Jerash, Jordan. The street is 600m (656.4yds) long and retains its original paving, which dates from the first century AD. Originally it would have been lined with a colonnade and shops

CURSUS PUBLICUS

A state postal service was founded during the republic and reorganised by Augustus. At first slaves and soldiers were used but Suetonius said that 'Augustus organised a chariot service based on posting stations – which proved to be a satisfactory arrangement because post-boys can be cross-examined on the situation as well as delivering written messages.' A relief on a tombstone in Belgrade shows a courier and driver in a light four-wheeled carriage drawn by two horses. His servant sits behind, back to the courier, holding a lance for their protection.

Frequent changes of horses enabled the couriers to make swift progress. Horses were changed at mansios (*mansiones*) usually placed between 32–48km (20–30 miles) apart but at shorter distances in difficult terrain. These were fitted with resting places, stables and bathhouses. Many later grew into small towns, such as that at Wall (Leocetum) on Watling Street. Progress of the couriers was usually 5m (7.4km) an hour and a courier would often cover 50m (75km) a day. Ordinary travellers who made use of these roads probably travelled about 20m (30km) a day or less. In AD 69 an imperial courier was sent from Mainz, then to Reims and then to Rome covering 2100km (1300 miles) in nine days. In AD 218 a journey from Rome to Aquileia (near Trieste) took three to four days over a distance of 750km (470 miles).

Senators could make use of the imperial post both for sending letters and for protection when travelling, providing they had a licence. These were prized and could be used on unofficial journeys; Pliny did so when he sent his wife by the courier service to visit her aunt, although he was careful to inform Trajan of what he had done. In contrast in AD 336 Libanius, a member of one of Antioch's distinguished families, was mortified to find that, having arrived at Constantinople, the man whom he had hoped would send him by imperial post to Athens had fallen from power and he was stranded.

In the third century Septimius Severus added the *cursus clabularis*, whose duty was to collect provisions for the army. For this purpose heavy wagons were used in addition to the ordinary carriages. It was then than the mansios expanded into towns as more people were needed to man these services. Inns had to put up government officials for free but could charge other travellers for their services.

SAFETY

Travelling was always hazardous and when possible people moved in groups. To try to protect travellers Augustus ordered that bandits should be executed; he stationed soldiers in bandit-ridden districts and Tiberius continued this practice. But the danger remained, as is shown by Pliny's letter to Baebius Hispanus, which recorded the disappearance of the equestrian Robustus on a journey in Umbria. The same thing had happened to his fellow townsman Metilius Crispus, for whom Pliny had acquired promotion to centurion. He had given him 40,000 sesterces for his outfit and equipment before he set out and Pliny speculated whether he had been killed by his slaves or along with them for the money. The mansios therefore provided places of shelter as well as rest on a journey. Pliny suggested that after the trials of a journey a traveller should take a walk and if possible a leisurely bath after being seated for a long time and this was certainly possible at a mansio.

Plutarch said that Cato sent his baker and his cook before him to find a place for a night's lodging. If no inn or friend were available he would seek out a local official to see what he could offer. Large inns with accommodation round a courtyard for stabling, eating places, rooms and latrines provided shelter as well as entertainment for a night, but in wilder places people would have to put up with what they could get. An inn on the Little St Bernard Pass consisted merely of a small stable and a courtyard building.

The wealthy always travelled with a large retinue both for protection and to show off their wealth. Horace ridiculed a praetor who travelled with 85 slaves, but Suetonius said that Nero seldom travelled without a train of less than a 1000 carriages, the mules shod with silver, the muleteers wearing Canusian wool and outriders with jingling bracelets and medallions escorting him. Claudius had his carriage fitted so that he could play games of dice and Commodus even had a carriage made with a swivelling seat so that it could be adjusted to catch a breeze or the sun depending on his wishes.

CARRIAGES

The cheapest form of transport was by pack animal. A mule might carry up to 300lbs (136kg), a horse up to 400lbs (182kg). Heavier loads had to be put in carts drawn by oxen. There were

several varieties of wheeled vehicles. A *plaustrum* was a two-wheeled cart drawn by two oxen; a *plaustrum maius* was a four-wheeled one drawn by four oxen. Both of these were mainly rural carts used for goods or passengers. Both Cato and Varro encouraged their use. Livy said that Hannibal requisitioned 2000 *plaustra* to supply his army in Italy. Loads could also be transported in a *currus*. A *benna* was a light carriage, which could be made of wickerwork. The *carrago* was a four-wheeled carriage or coach, which was developed during the empire. It could be expensive. Martial mentioned a gilt coach might cost the price of a farm. An *esseda* had been developed as a war chariot in Gaul but was used by the Romans for sham fights. A *sarracum* was a four-wheeled chariot used for campaigns but also for carrying building material. The *biga*, a light two-wheeled vehicle and the *quadriga*, a four-wheeled vehicle were both used in chariot races, while a *triga* was a two-wheeled chariot with three horses, one being attached by a rein to run by the side of the other two.

A *raeda* was a carriage used by the elite. It was this vehicle which Juvenal complained was disturbing his sleep. A *carpentum* was a two-wheeled vehicle used mainly by women with a canopy supported by four columns. Curtains would hide the occupant from view. Both these groups would use a litter when in a town to avoid the muddy streets and mixing with the crowds. Augustus liked this method of transport so much that he used it to go to Tivoli even though this took him two days. Some people regarded a litter as being effeminate but Juvenal said that it did at least allow one to sleep or read. Suetonius said that Caligula became so self indulgent that he travelled in a litter drawn by eight horses and, whenever he approached a town, he made the inhabitants sweep the roads and lay the dust with sprinklers.

Drawing of a four-wheeled wagon, possibly a version of a plaustrum, from a funerary monument near Trier

HORACE'S JOURNEY

One journey, recorded in detail, is that which Horace made from Rome to Brundisium in 38 BC as a member of an embassy of Maecenas. He set out with a friend, Heliodorus, in a carriage along the Appian Way and stayed the night at Aricia in a 'modest inn'. The second day he went to Forum Appia where he transferred to a barge towed by a mule through the Pontine Marshes to Terracina. This was overnight but Horace got no sleep because 'murderous mosquitoes' plagued him, frogs croaked and a sailor sang to his girlfriend. The boat was also delayed as the sailor unhitched the mule and had a sleep on the bank, until roused by a furious passenger. Horace stayed at Terracina to meet Maecenas. The next day the company moved to Formiae where they stayed in a comfortable villa owned by a friend of Maecenas. Here they remained for the next day when Virgil joined the party. The following day they moved on, spending that night in a simple inn at Sinuessa and the next at Capua. More comfortable conditions were provided on the next evening, when they stayed at Caudium in a huge villa owned by one of the officials in the party and their dinner ended with entertainment by two professional comics.

It was on the following night when they stayed at an inn at Beneventum that the innkeeper, while turning thrushes over a fire, set light to the roof. Scared servants and famished diners tried to save their dinners while everyone else tried to extinguish the flames. The next night at a little inn in the Apennines the fire smoked causing his eyes to water. He hoped for a girl to stay with him but 'the cheating girl' never came.

The party moved on, this time in wagons, to stay at the small town of Asculum Apulum, which had good bread but foul water, so travellers took bread with them to the next night stay at Canusium, where the bread was gritty. The next day they went through heavy rain to Rubi. After a good night's rest they made their way over bad roads to stay one night at Bari and the next at Egnatia. Finally on the sixteenth day after leaving Rome and having travelled over 595km (370 miles) Horace arrived at Brundisium, 'the end of a long journey'.

INLAND WATERWAYS

River transport was important. The Tiber was navigable throughout most of the year and this was vital for transporting grain from Ostia to Rome. Pliny in a letter to Domitius Apollinaris said that goods could be shipped down the Tiber from his Tuscan villa in winter and spring but not in summer when its dry bed appeared. Elsewhere in the empire, rivers such as the Rhine, the Rhone and the Danube made natural waterways.

Canals were constructed where possible. Nero had a scheme to make a canal from Lake Avernus on the Bay of Naples to Rome but this was never completed. Possibly if the canal had been built it would have to have gone through the Pontine Marshes, thus helping to drain them and prevent the misery of mosquitoes, which so infuriated Horace. Domitian replaced Nero's canal by a road. Another abortive canal was that suggested between the Saône and the Moselle, which would have allowed goods arriving from the Mediterranean and up the Rhone to pass via the Moselle to the Rhine and thus to the North Sea, but Aelius Gracilis, Governor of Gallia Belgica, stopped this, fearing that it might bring a rival group into his territory. A canal was built from Ravenna to the River Po, which proved successful and others were added in the Po

valley and along the Adriatic coast. Pliny, when Governor of Bithynia had suggested a canal to Trajan. Development of canals, however, was mainly local and sparse; the Romans preferred to rely on road transport.

SEA TRANSPORT

The Romans were wary of the sea. Hazards included going aground, piracy, storms and shipwrecks; St Paul was shipwrecked on Malta when he sailed for Rome. There were no compasses, sextants or other aids to navigation. Usually ships kept close to the coast so that they could use mountains and other sites as aids. At night they used the stars. Lighthouses, such as that at Dover, were placed on the coast. Ships relied on steering oars; rudders were not invented until later. Julius Caesar secured a triumph by crossing Oceanus to Britain and twice returning relatively unscathed, although each time he had been caught by unexpected tides and storms in the English Channel. The Romans confined themselves to coastal shipping and to the Mediterranean. Even then passages were not available all year. The main sailing season was May to October. Apuleius said that in some parts of the Mediterranean a religious feast marked the opening of the season. Certainly sacrifices were made before a ship sailed and after its safe arrival.

Mosaic showing a lighthouse, possibly that at the mouth of Claudian's harbour, and a ship with one sail and a steering oar. The inscription navi (cularii) Narbonenses indicates that the shipping agent in this office was engaged in trade from Narbo, Gaul. (Square of the Corporations, Ostia)

Ostia was one of the ports receiving beasts for the amphitheatre. This mosaic may indicate that this shipping agent dealt with this trade or that he was engaged in the ivory trade, which was organised from Sabrata. (Square of the Corporations, Ostia)

The most important trade was that which brought Rome its grain from Egypt, but shipping also brought marble from Asia Minor and wine and oil from Gaul and Spain. Passengers were taken, but Cicero indicated their wariness of the sea when he sailed in 51 BC to take up his post as governor of Cilicia. He left Athens on 6 July, sailed though the Aegean with frequent stops and finally arrived at Ephesus on 22 July but every night he slept on land. Usually distances were measured by days. Rome to Narbonne was estimated as three days and Rome to Alexandria as 10 days. The speed of a voyage was dependent on the weather, the direction of the wind and the ability of the sailors to secure the fastest passage.

At Ostia shipping officers could give information about sailings on a regular basis, probably because of the numerous ships using that port. Evidence from the Square of the Corporations at Ostia indicates that shipping facilities were well organised both for passengers and for freight. Small offices probably held representatives of shipping companies from which orders and collections could be made. Passengers could book passages there. In front of each office a mosaic floor indicated the trade of the *navicularii* or *negotiarii*. The two harbours would have provided excellent shipping facilities.

People went to shipping masters' offices, asked for the next sailing and negotiated a passage with the ship's master or even with the crew, then awaited shouts from a ship that it was about to sail. There were no set times. Sailings depended on the tides, winds, weather and avoiding

A boatman carries an amphora from a merchant vessel to a river craft. (Square of the Corporations, Ostia)

ill-omened days. Sacrifices had to be made to Neptune or Poseidon and if there were bad omens the sailing was postponed. Sailors' superstitions played a part. Sneezing on a gangplank and bad dreams could cause delay.

Travellers had other problems. Ships had accommodation for officers and crew and could find accommodation for important guests. Ordinary passengers had to bed down where they could, even if it was on deck. If they were lucky they secured a place under a tent-like structure put up at night and taken down each morning. They had to take their own bedding and food as well as the goods they wished to transport. Crews were only employed to look after the ship, not to look after passengers' needs, so these had to arrange everything themselves. Some travellers had slaves to arrange these details, and bribes and threats would ensure their masters' comfort. Frequent callings at ports ensured that food could be bought during the voyage and cooked, for a price, in the ship's galley.

Passengers had to make the best of it – telling tales, gambling, reading, and watching the seamen – anything to relieve the monotony. Important passengers could chat to the captain sitting on chair on the poop deck and watch him navigate the ship. If there were problems everyone was called on to help. St Paul on his voyage was called on to dump tackle and then the cargo of grain. Once port had been reached and the tugs had rowed the ship to its berth sacrifices were made for a safe arrival and to ensure that the next voyage would be equally safe.

SMALL CRAFTS

These were used in harbours and on rivers. They were needed to tow vessels to the quayside and as lighters to transfer goods from ships to the docks. Skippers of these crafts probably checked documents of arriving ships and allocated their berths. A tomb relief from Isola Sacra near Ostia shows a boat being rowed by three men with a towline going from the boat to a large vessel out of sight beyond the relief, and apparently towing the larger boat to dock either at Ostia or Rome. Dionysius mentioned ships laden with 3000 amphorae unloading in Rome and warships could make the journey with their superior rowing power. Even so the Tiber was a difficult river on which to row or to sail. Procopius, in the sixth century AD, said that cargoes were reloaded at Ostia into barges, which were drawn by oxen 'like wagons to Rome.' Other rivers were more navigable. Reliefs show cargo being transferred down the Moselle. Seneca mentioned pleasure boats and houseboats; boats were not only used for industrial purposes. Studies of mosaics, tombstones and reliefs have revealed a variety of vessels with specialist functions.

Every area of the empire had its own method of building these boats. Julius Caesar said that the Veneti, a Gallic tribe, built oak ships with flat bottoms, high prows and sterns. Their sails were of hide or softened leather. These could go through shallow depth at low tides.

Close up of the steersman on the Neumagen funerary monument. Boats of this kind regularly plied along the Rhine and the Moselle. (Rheinisches Landesmuseum, Trier)

MERCHANT VESSELS

Merchant galleys were used to carry dispatches as well as passengers and cargo and were marked as such by a goose head. They might have sails or oars, which were used to get ships into harbour. Rowers were not slaves; that is a modern myth. Admittedly these were sometimes fugitives from justice, but others had been manumitted before they became rowers or they came from the provinces. The crew often had to bail water. Lucian said that a bad captain would put a cowardly sailor in command of the ship and his best sailor in the bilge to ensure the water was bailed, although other writers felt that being in the bilge was a punishment. A good ship used an Archimedean screw or a treadmill to get rid of the water.

Merchant ships carried bulky goods – grain, stone, marble and amphorae. Ships carrying grain not only escaped paying taxes but also avoided being commandeered by the military. Ships could be constructed for special purposes. One was built, on Caligula's order to transport an obelisk weighing 322 tonnes and a base weighing 174 tonnes from Egypt to Rome. This obelisk now stands in St Peter's Square. This huge ship, 104m (340ft) long and 20.3m (64ft) wide, was sunk to provide a foundation for the lighthouse at the Claudian harbour at Ostia.

Larger vessels copied warships, giving themselves a sternpost with a figure on top. Ships were given names of mythological personages and emperors. These ships could be commandeered when required for a military campaign, as Caesar did for his invasions of Britain. Ships could be huge. In the second century AD Lucian was told that a grain ship had been blown off course and was taking shelter in Piraeus. Having walked five miles from Athens to Piraeus he described it as being 55m (180 ft) long, 14m (45ft) wide and 13m (44ft) from the deck to the bottom of the hull. The stern rose to a gilded goose head; the forward prow had a figure of Isis. This may have been a *corbita*, a ship specially built to carry grain, at least 1000 tons, which Lucian remarked could feed Athens for a year. Lucian marvelled at its size and at the crew 'like an army'. A little old man controlled the ship with a tiller 'no more than a stick'.

KINGS AND EMPERORS

KINGS

Romulus	753–715 BC
Numa Pompilius	715–673
Tullus Hostilius	673–642
Ancus Martius	642–617
Tarquinius Priscus	616–579
Servius Tullius	578–535
Tarquinius Superbus	534–509

EMPERORS

Augustus	27 BC–AD 14	Marcus Aurelius	161–180 } Joint reign
Tiberius	14–37	Lucius Verus	161–169
Caligula	37–41	Commodus	180–192
Claudius	41–54	Pertinax	193 January–March
Nero	54–68	Didius Julius	193 March–June
Galba	68–69	Septimius Severus	193–211
Otho	69	Geta	211 February–December } Joint reign
Vitellius	69	Caracalla	211–217
Vespasian	69–79	Macrinus	217–218
Titus	79–81	Elagabalus	218–222
Domitian	81–96	Alexander Severus	222–235
Nerva	96–98	Maximinus	235–238
Trajan	98–117	Gordian I	238 March–April
Hadrian	117–138	Gordian II	238 March–April
Antoninus Pius	138–161		

Pupienus	238 April–July	
Gordian III	238–244	
Philip	244–249	
Decius	249–251	
Trebonianus	251–253	
Aemilianus	253 August–October	
Valerianus	253–260	
Gallienus	260–268	
Claudius II	268–270	
Quintillus	270 August–September	
Aurelian	270–275	
Tacitus	275–276	
Florianus	276 July–September	
Probus	276–282	
Carus	282–283	} Joint reign
Carinus	283–285	

Numerianus	283–284	
Diocletian	284–305	
Maximian	286–305	} Division of
Constantius I	305–306	the empire
Galerius	305–311}	
Licinius	311–324}	
Constantine	106–337	
Constantine II	337–340	} Civil War
Constans	337–350	
Constantius II	337–361	
Julian	361–363	
Jovian	363–364	
Valentinian I	364–375	} Joint reign
Valens	364–378	
Gratian	375–383	} Joint reign
Valentinian II	375–392	

EASTERN EMPIRE

Theodosius I	379–395
Theodosius II	408–450
Marcian	450–457

WESTERN EMPIRE

Arcadius	395–408
Honorius	395–423
Valentinian III	423–455

CLASSICAL AUTHORS MENTIONED IN THE TEXT

Ammianus Marcellinus (*c*.AD 330–395). Roman historian, who was a Greek native of Antioch, became an officer to the Roman general Ursicinus in 354. He joined the Emperor Julian's invasion of Persia in 363 and later visited Egypt and Greece. In the late 380s he wrote a history of Rome continuing the history of Tacitus from AD 69 to his own day. The first 13 books have been lost; the remainder cover the years 354–378.

Anon. The *Periplus maris Erythraei* is the work of an anonymous Greek traveller of the first century AD describing the coasts of the Red Sea and the Arabian Gulf, as well as showing knowledge of parts of India and East Africa.

Anon. Author of the *Moretum*, one of a group of short Latin poems in a collection called *Appendix Virgilana* dating from around the time of Virgil. *The Moretum* or *The Salad* deals with a peasant's preparation in the early morning of his meal, then setting out for the day's work.

Anthimus (active AD 474–511). A Greek doctor who was attached to the court of Emperor Zeno. He became involved in treacherous activities and fled to the court of Theodosius, who sent him on a diplomatic mission to the Franks. Some time after AD 511 he wrote a handbook on dietetics *De Observatione Ciborum Theodoricum Regem Francorum Epistula*, half medical text, half cookery book.

Apuleius (active *c*.AD 155). *Metamorphoses* or the *Golden Ass* is the one Latin novel which survives in its entirety and gives many details of popular life. The hero is accidentally turned into an ass and has a series of adventures.

Aristotle (384–322 BC). Greek philosopher who taught in Athens at the Academy. His works cover every branch of philosophy and science known in his day and had a great influence of late antiquity and subsequent eras.

Aulus Gellius (*c.*AD 130–?180). Author of *Noctes Atticae* (*Attic Nights*) a collection of short accounts based on his readings from Greek and Roman texts. These deal with a variety of subjects but is a mine of information from Greek and Roman authors and on customs.

Caesar (100–44 BC). Roman statesman, general and dictator. He subdued Gaul between 61 and 56 BC and invaded Britain twice in 55 and 54 BC. His *De Bello Gallico* (*Commentaries on the Gallic Wars*) is written in the third person to indicate his belief that it is an objective, truthful record of events.

Cato (234–149 BC). Roman statesman and moralist. His literary works included *Origines*, a history of the origins of Rome and the Italian cities, together with the more recent Punic wars. His *De Re Rustica*, also known as *De Agri Cultura*, is concerned mainly with the cultivation of fruits, olives and vines. He wrote from his own experience and was mainly concerned with the practical necessities of running an estate.

Celsius (lived during the reign of Tiberius). A writer of eight books on medicine and medical science, diet, the treatment of diseases and surgery. His work was rediscovered in the fifteenth century and remained a useful textbook until the nineteenth century.

Cicero (106–43 BC). Roman statesman and orator, whose prolific writing included poems, letters and prosecution and defence speeches. Many of his numerous letters were to his friend Atticus. His political career included the governorship of Cilicia.

Columella (active AD 60–65). A Spaniard who served in the Roman army, he composed a treatise on farming, *De Re Rustica*. This covered all aspects of running an estate including livestock, cultivation, gardens and the duties of a bailiff and his wife.

Dio Cassius (*c.*AD 150–235). Also known as Cassius Dio. A Roman historian, born in Bithynia, and governor of Dalmatia and Africa. He wrote a history of the civil war, 193–97 (now lost) and a history of Rome in 80 books. This begins with the coming of Aeneas to Italy after the Sack of Troy and ends in AD 229. Much of the part after AD 9 has been lost, but what remains is useful, especially his contemporary comments on the third century.

Dionysius of Halicarnassus (first century BC). Greek historian who lived in Rome and wrote treatises of criticism and philosophy. His 20 volumes on Roman Antiquaries gave the history of Rome to 264 BC.

Diodorus Siculus (active *c.*60–39 BC). A Greek historian who wrote a world history in 40 books centred on Rome. These are based on ancient sources and are a useful but uncritical compilation of legends, social history and mythology. He was first to write on the medical use of plants.

Florus (second century AD). Latin historian, probably a friend of Hadrian, who wrote a history of Rome up to the age of Augustus.

Frontinus (c.AD 30–c.AD 104). After serving as consul in AD 73 or 74, he was Governor of Britain 74–78. He wrote *Strategemata*, a manual on war strategies for the use of officers and *De Aquis Urbis Romae*, dealing with the history, technicalities and the regulation of the aqueducts of Rome.

Fronto (c.AD 100–c.176). Roman orator who was born in North Africa but spent much of his life in Rome and was tutor to Marcus Aurelius and Lucius Verus. He wrote a collection of letters that were discovered in the nineteenth century.

Galen (AD 129–199). Born in Pergamum. A Greek physician who rose from a gladiator doctor in Asia Minor to court physician to the Emperors Marcus Aurelius, Commodus and Septimius Severus. He lectured, demonstrated and wrote on every aspect of medicine and anatomy. His books had enormous influence and formed the basis of many later medical works.

Herodian (active c.AD 230). An historian, born in Syria, who wrote the *Historia Augusta*, a history in eight books from the death of Marcus Aurelius (AD 180) to the accession of Gordian III (AD 238).

Hippocrates (c.460–c.370 BC). Probably the most famous figure in Greek medicine whose name is attached to the Hippocratic Corpus, 60 treatises dealing with medicine, surgery and health.

Horace (65–8 BC). Roman poet, all of whose published work survives. The *Epodes* and the *Satires* were written about 30 BC and the *Odes* in 23 BC. He also wrote the *Epistles* and *Carmen Saeculare*, the latter dealing with the Secular Games of 17 BC.

Josephus (AD 37–after 93). Jewish historian who wrote a history of the Jewish Revolt against Rome, which began in AD 66. The work contains one of the best descriptions of the Roman army.

Juvenal (active second century AD). He was probably the greatest of the Roman satirical poets, writing 16 bitter, humorous *Satires* portraying life in second-century Rome.

Livy (59 BC–AD 17). He was born in Padua and is the author of the *History of Rome* in 142 books, the last 22 of which dealt with events in his own time.

Lucian of Samosata (c.AD 120–180). Traveller and lecturer who moved to Athens and developed public recitations. Later he moved to Egypt.

Lucretius (c.99–c.55 BC). Roman poet and philosopher. Author of *De Rerum Natura*, a poem dealing with the system of Epicurus and demonstrating that fear of the gods was groundless and that the world and everything in it was governed by the mechanical laws of nature.

Martial (*c*.AD 40–103). A Spaniard who worked in Rome after AD 64 and relied on his poetry for a living. Between AD 86 and 98 he wrote 11 books of *Epigrams*, short poems each of which pithily expressed a concept with the subject matter ranging across the spectrum of Roman life.

Oribasius (*c*.AD 320–390s). Born in Pergamum and became physician to the emperor Julian around AD 351. At the emperor's request he wrote four books of *Medical Compilations* taking extracts from Galen, Athenaeus, Rufus, Diocles and other writers. After the emperor's death in 361 he moved to the court of the emperor Theodosius and wrote two abridgements of his work.

Ovid (43 BC–AD 17). A poet, born in the valley of the Apennines, east of Rome, who travelled round the Mediterranean. His poetry aroused the displeasure of the Imperial court and he was banished to Tomis on the Black Sea. His main poems are the *Ars Amatoria, Tristia, Fasti* and *Metamorphoses*.

Palladius (active fourth century AD). A Latin author whose main treatise on agriculture, *De Re Rustica*, in 14 books contains general information on setting up and managing a farm and the work to be done each month.

Persius (AD 34–54). Flaccus Persius was an uncompromising stoic who wrote letters satirising characters, who are either aged or immature tutors and students.

Petronius (died *c*.AD 69). A Roman satirical writer and author of the *Satyricon*, a novel of which the most well known part is Trimalchio's feast, an ostentatious dinner party to which a motley crowd are invited as guests or gain admittance.

Plautus (*c*.250–184 BC). A Roman dramatist born in Umbria, he wrote about 130 comedies of which 29 have survived. Although having many stock characters, the plays deal with contemporary life and social settings.

Pliny the Elder (AD 23/24–79). A prolific writer on natural history, his 37 books cover most aspects of natural history, ranging through natural phenomena, medicine, botany, zoology, geography and minerals. His nephew recorded his death during the eruption of Vesuvius.

Pliny the Younger (AD 61–112). He was adopted by his maternal uncle, Pliny the Elder, and became an administrator, holding several offices of state, including that of Governor of Bithynia-Pontus on the Black Sea, where he died. He wrote a large number of letters, which cover a wide variety of subjects, personal and official.

Plutarch (*c*.AD 50–129). Mestrius Plutarchus of Chaeronea visited Athens, Egypt and Italy and eventually lectured at Rome. For 30 years he was a priest at Delphi. He wrote over 200 books including a group of rhetorical works, a series of dialogues of Roman questions and Greek questions dealing with religious antiquities. He also wrote *Parallel Lives* exemplifying the virtues and vices of famous men.

Polybius (*c*.200–118 BC). A Greek historian who lived in Rome, and wrote a history of Greece in 40 books, covering the period 264–146 BC. He focused on military and political affairs and provided eye witness accounts of events.

Procopius (AD 500–after 562). A Byzantine-Greek historian and secretary to Belisarius, general to Justinian. His *History of the Wars of Justinian*, AD 527–553 is a clear and reliable account of these years and the main source of the first part of Justinian's reign.

Quintilian (*c*.AD 35–? *c*. late first century AD). Born in Spain he moved to Rome to become a teacher of rhetoric. He was tutor to a number of emperors but retired in AD 808 to write books on oratory and the teaching of oratory, which Martial declared to be the 'supreme guide of wayward youth'.

Seneca the Younger (*c*.4 BC–AD 65). Roman politician, philosopher and dramatist, who was born at Corduba in Spain and came to Rome to study rhetoric and philosophy before setting out on a political career. He was chief advisor to Nero but in 65 was implicated in the conspiracy of Piso and forced to commit suicide. He wrote voluminously on many subjects including rhetoric and philosophy. His *Naturales Quaestiones* dealt with natural phenomena. He also wrote 20 books of *Epistulae Morales ad Lucilium*, an artificial correspondence.

Sidonius Apollinaris (*c*.AD 430–*c*.480). A Gallo-Roman poet, born in Lyons, who became Bishop of Augustonemetum (Clemont-Ferrand) and a major figure in classical culture. He published nine books of letters, many detailing life and conditions in Gaul in the fifth century AD.

Silius Italicus (*c*.AD 26–101). Latin poet and lawyer who became governor of Asis *c*.AD 77. When he retired to Rome he wrote poetry.

Soranus (second century AD). One of the greatest Greek physicians, who studied in Alexandria and practised in Rome during the reigns of Trajan and Hadrian. He wrote 20 books on medicine and terminological problems. Two of his works have survived in their entirety, a treatise on fractures and another on gynaecology.

Statius (*c*.AD 45–*c*.96). A Roman poet, born in Naples, who moved to Rome and recited his poems to an admiring audience. He published two works on classical mythology.

Strabo (64–after 24 BC). A Greek geographer who came to Rome several times after 44 BC and travelled widely round the Mediterranean. His 17 books, the *Geography*, cover the chief provinces of Roman world and other inhabited regions round the Mediterranean.

Suetonius (born *c*.69 BC). He wrote widely on antiquities and natural sciences, but the work that survives is his *Lives of the Caesars*, an account of Julius Caesar and the 11 subsequent emperors.

Tacitus (AD 56–c.117). Born in Gaul, he eventually became a Roman senator and Governor of Asia. He married Agricola's daughter and wrote a life of his father-in-law, published in AD 98, which gives a much-quoted description of Britain. In the same year he wrote the *Germania* dealing with the history and customs of the German tribes, north of the Rhine and the Danube. His major works, the *Histories*, dealing with the period AD 69–96, and the *Annals*, covering the period AD 14–68, are invaluable for the events of the first century AD.

Tertullian (c.AD 160–220). A Latin Christian writer who was born in Carthage and trained as a lawyer. He converted to Christianity about AD 195 and then devoted himself to Christian writings including defending the Church against charges of atheism and magic.

Tibullus (c.55–19 BC). Roman poet who was a friend of Ovid and Horace. He wrote two books of elegies, concerned with love and the pleasures of country life.

Valerius Maximus (early first century AD). A Roman historian who accompanied Sextus Pomponius, the younger son of Pompey, to Asia in AD 27. On his return he wrote nine books of historical examples illustrating moral and philosophical points mainly drawn from Cicero and Livy.

Varro (116–27 BC). A prolific writer who is said to have written over 600 books. Of these probably the most important were *De Lingua Latina*, a treatise on Latin grammar, and *De Re Rustica*, in three books, which was intended as a practical manual of running a farm for the benefit of his wife, Fundania.

Vegetius (active c.AD 379–395). A military writer who wrote a manual, *Epitoma Rei Militaris*, on military training and the organisation of a Roman legion.

Virgil (70–19 BC). Roman poet born in Cisalpine Gaul, who studied philosophy in Rome. About 42 BC he began the composition of the *Eclogues* while he was living in the Campania. This was followed by the *Georgics* and the *Aeneid*. After his death he was regarded as one of the greatest of the Latin poets and his works and his tomb outside Naples became the objects of a cult.

Vitruvius (first century BC). Roman engineer and architect who saw military service under Julius Caesar. His treatise in 10 books, *De Architectura* (*On Architecture*) covering civil, military and domestic architecture, building materials, interior decoration, water supplies and the qualifications for architects was compiled from his own experience and from works of other architects. It had immense influence during the Renaissance.

BIBLIOGRAPHY

Adkins, L. and Adkins, R. A. *Dictionary of Roman Religion*. Oxford: Oxford University Press 2000.

Alcock, J. P. *Food in the Ancient World*. Westport CT: Greenwood Press 2005.

Ashby, T. *The Aqueducts of Ancient Rome*. Oxford: Oxford University Press 1935.

Ando, C. (ed.) *Roman Religion*. Edinburgh: Edinburgh University Press 2003.

Baillie-Reynolds, P. K. *The Vigiles of Imperial Rome*. London: Oxford University Press 1926.

Balsdon, J. P. V. D. *Roman Women: their History and Habits*. London: Bodley Head 1962.

Balsdon, J. P. V. D. *Life and Leisure in Ancient Rome*. London: Bodley Head 1969.

Balsdon, J. P. V. D. *Romans and Aliens*. London: Duckworth 1979.

Barbet, A. *La Peinture Murale Romaine, les styles décoratifs pompéiens*. Paris: Picard 1985.

Bauman, R. A. *Women and Politics in Ancient Rome*. London and New York: Routledge 1992.

Beacham, R. C. *The Roman Theatre and its Audience*. London and New York: Routledge 1991.

Beard, M. *The Roman Triumph*. Cambridge Mas.: London: Belknap Press of Harvard University 2007.

Beard, M. *Pompeii: The Life and Death of a Roman Town*. London: Profile 2008.

Blackman, D. R., and Hodge, A. T. *Frontinus' Legacy. Essays on Frontinus' de Aquis Urbis Romae*. Ann Arbor: University of Michigan Press 2004.

Boatwright, M. T., Gargola, D. J. and Talbert, P. J. A. *A Brief History of the Romans*. Oxford: Oxford University Press 2006.

Boppert, W. *Zivile Grabsteine aus Mainz und Umgebung. Corpus Signorum Imperii Romani. Deutshland II.6*. Mainz: Römanische-Germanischen Zentralmuseuems 1992

Boyce, G. K. Corpus of the Lararia of Pompeii. Rome: *American Academy in Rome* 1937.

Bradley, K. *Slaves and Masters in the Roman Empire: a Study in Social Control*. Oxford: Oxford University Press 1987.

Bradley, K. *Slavery and Society at Rome*. Cambridge: Cambridge University Press 1994.

Braund, D. (ed.) *The Administration of the Roman Empire 241 BC–AD 193*. Exeter: University of Exeter Press 1988.

Briquel, D. 'Les Femmes Gladiateurs: examen du dossier'. *Ktema* 17. 1992, 47–53.

Brunt, P. A. and Moore, J. M. *Res Gestae Divi Augusti: the Achievements of the Divine Augustus*. Oxford: Oxford University Press 1967.

Burford, A. *Craftsmen in Greek and Roman Society*. London: Thames and Hudson 1972.

Burnett, A. *Coinage in the Roman World*. London: Seaby 1987.

Cameron, A. *Circus Factions*. Oxford: Clarendon Press 1976.

Campbell, B. *The Roman Army: a Sourcebook*. London and New York: Routledge 1990.

Carcopino., J. *Daily Life in Ancient Rome*. London: Routledge and Kegan Paul 1941.

Carroll-Spilleck, M. *Spirits of the Dead: Roman Funerary Commemoration in Western Europe*. Oxford: Oxford University Press 2006.

Cary, M. and Scullard, H. H. *A History of Rome* 3rd edit. New York: St Martins Press 1975.

Casson, L. *Ships and Seamanship in the Roman World*. Princeton: Princeton University Press 1971.

Casson, L. *Travel in the Roman World*. London: George Allen and Unwin 1974.

Chase, R. G. *Ancient Hellenistic and Roman Amphitheatres, Stadiums and Theatres: The way they look now*. Portsmouth N.H.: P. E. Randall 2002.

Chevallier, R. *Voyages et Désplacements dans l'Empire Romain*. Paris: Armand Colin 1988.

Chevallier, R. *Roman Roads*. Translated by N. H. Field. London: Batsford 1989.

Claridge, A. *Rome. Oxford Archaeological Guide*. Oxford: Oxford University Press 1998.

Clarke, J. R. *Roman Black-and-White Figural Mosaics*. New York: New York University Press 1979.

Clarke, J. R. *The Houses of Roman Italy 100 BC–AD 250: Ritual, Space and Decoration:* Berkeley: University of California Press 1991.

Coleman, K. M. 'Fatal Charades: Roman Executions Staged as Mythological Enactments.' *Journal of Roman Studies* 80.1990, 44-73.

Connolly, P. *Colosseum. Rome's Arena of Death*. London: BBC Books 2003.

Connolly, P. and Dodge, H. *The Ancient City. Life in Classical Athens and Rome*. Oxford: Oxford University Press 1998.

Cornell, T. J. *The Beginnings of Rome*. London: Routledge and Kegan Paul 1995.

Cornell, T. and Matthews, J. *Atlas of the Roman World*. London: Phaidon 1982.

Cowen, R. *For the Glory of Rome. A History of Warriors and Warfare*. London: Greenhill Books 2007.

Crook, J. A. *Law and Life of Ancient Rome*. London: Thames and Hudson 1967.

Croom, A. T. *Roman Clothing and Fashion*. Stroud: Tempus Publishing 2000.

Croom, A. T. *Roman Furniture*. Tempus Publishing 2007.

Cruse, A. *Roman Medicine*. Stroud: Tempus Publishing 2004.

Cuoma, S. *Technology and Culture in the Roman World*. Cambridge: Cambridge University Press 2007.

D'Ambra, E. *Art and Identity in the Roman World*. London: Weidenfeld and Nicolson 1998.

D'Ambra, E. *Roman Women*. Cambridge: Cambridge University Press 2007.

D'Arms, J. H. and Koff, E. C. (eds) *The Seaborne Commerce of Ancient Rome*. Rome: American Academy in Rome, 36 1980.

DeLaine, J. and Johnston, D. E. (eds) *Roman Baths and Bathing. Proceedings of the First International Conference on Roman Baths held at Bath, England*. Journal of Roman Archaeology Supplementary Series No. 37 1992.

Dilke, O. A. W. 'The Roman Surveyors'. *Greece and Rome* 9 1962 170-180.

Dilke, O. A. W. *The Roman Land Surveyors. An Introduction to the Agrimensores*, Newton Abbot: David and Charles 1971.

Dixon, S. *The Roman Family*. Baltimore: John Hopkins University Press 1992.

Dixon, S. *Reading Roman Women*. London: Duckworth 2001.

Dobbins, L. J. and Foss, P. W. (eds) *The World of Pompeii*. London and New York: Routledge 2007.

Dowden, K. *Religion and the Romans*. London: Bristol Classical Press 1992.

Drinkwater, J. F. *Roman Gaul: the Three Provinces 58 BC–AD 260*. London: Croom Helm 1993.

Du Prey, P de la R. *The Villas of Pliny the Younger from Antiquity to Posterity*. Chicago: University of Chicago Press 1994.

Dudley, D. *Urbs Romana. A Source Book of Classical Texts on the City and its Monuments*. London: Phaidon Press 1967.

Dunbabin, K. M. *The Roman Banquet. Images of Conviviality*. Cambridge: Cambridge University Press 2003.

Duncan-Jones, R. *The Economy of the Roman Empire: Quantitative Studies.* Cambridge: Cambridge University Press 1974.

Dupont, F. *Daily Life in Ancient Rome.* Translated by C. Woodall. Oxford: Blackwell 1989.

Ellis, S. P. *Roman Housing.* London: Duckworth 2000.

Emery, G. T. 'Dental Pathology and Archaeology'. *Antiquity.* 37. 1963, 274–281.

Engels, D. 'The Problems of Female Infanticide in the Graeco-Roman World'. *Classical Philology.* 75. 1980, 112-120.

Erdcamp, P (ed.). *Companion to the Roman Army.* Oxford: Blackwell 2007.

Fagan, G. G. *Bathing in Public in the Roman World.* Ann Arbor: University of Michigan Press 1999.

Favro, D. *The Urban Image of Augustan Rome.* Cambridge: Cambridge University Press 1996.

Finley, M.I. *The Ancient Economy.* Berkeley: University of California Press 1973.

Finley, M.I. *Ancient Slavery and Modern Ideology.* London: Chatto and Windus 1980.

M. I Finley (ed.) *Studies in Ancient Society.* London and New York: Routledge 1989.

Ferguson, J. *The Religions of the Roman Empire.* London: Thames and Hudson 1970.

Frazer, A. (ed.) *Villa Urbana.* Philadelphia: University Museum Monograph 101 Symposium Series A. University Museum, University of Pennsylvania 1998.

Freis, H. *Die Cohortes Urbanae.* Koln: Bohlau 1967.

Futrell, A. *The Roman Games: A Sourcebook.* Oxford: Blackwell 2005.

Gardner, J. F. and Wiedemann, T. *The Roman Household: a Sourcebook.* London and New York: Routledge, 1991.

Gagé, J. *Les Classes Sociales dans l'Empire Romain.* Paris: Payot 1971.

Garnsey, P. *Social Status and Legal Privilege in the Roman Empire.* Oxford: Clarendon Press 1970.

Garnsey, P. *Food and Society in Classical Antiquity.* Cambridge: Cambridge University Press 1999.

Gernsey, P. *Famine and Food Supply in the Graeco-Roman World: Responses to Risk and Crisis.* Cambridge: Cambridge University Press 1988.

Garnsey, P. Hopkins, K and Whittaker, C. R. (eds) *Trade in the Ancient Economy.* London: Chatto and Windus 1983.

Garnsey, P. and Saller, R. *The Roman Empire: Economy, Society and Culture.* London: Duckworth 1987.

Gibbon, E. *The Decline and Fall of the Roman Empire.* London: David and Charles 1993.

Golden, M. 'Did the Romans care when their children died?' *Greece and Rome* 32. 2. 1988, 152-163.

Golden, M. *Sport in the Ancient World from A to Z.* London and New York: Routledge 2004.

Golvin, J-C. and Landes, C. *Amphitheatres and Gladiators.* Presses de CNRS: Inst. Grafico Bertello 1990.

Gordon, R. L. 'Mithraeism and Roman Society. Social Factors in the Explanation of Religious Change in the Roman Empire'. *Religion* 2.2. 1972, 92–121.

Graham, E-J. *Death, Disposal and the Destitute: The Burial of the Urban Poor in Italy in the Late Roman Republic and Early Empire.* British Archaeological Reports. Int. Series 1565. Archaeopress 2007.

Grant, M. *Gladiators.* London: Weidenfeld and Nicolson 1967.

Grant. M. *Cities of Vesuvius: Pompeii and Herculaneum.* London: Weidenfeld and Nicholson 1971.

Grant, M. *History of Rome.* London: Weidenfeld and Nicolson 1978.

Greene, K. *The Archaeology of the Roman Economy.* London: Batsford 1986.

Grimal, P. *Les Jardins Romains.* Paris: Presses Universitaires de France 1969.

Hatt, J. J. *La Tombe Gallo-Romaine.* Patis: Picard 2000.

Hales, S. *The Roman House and Social Identity.* Cambridge: Cambridge University Press 2003.

Harney, L. A. *The Roman Engineers.* Cambridge: Cambridge University Press 1981.

Harris, W. V. 'Child-exposure in the Roman Empire', *Journal of Roman Studies,* 54. 1994, 1–22.

Healy, J. F. *Mining and Metallurgy in the Roman World.* London: Thames and Hudson 1978.

Hermansen, G. *Ostia: Aspects of Roman City Life.* Edmonton: University of Alberta Press 1982.

Hodge, A. T. *Roman Aqueducts and Water Supply.* 2nd edit. London: Duckworth 2002.

Hope, V. M. *Death in Ancient Rome: a Sourcebook.* London and New York: Routledge 2007.

Hope, V. M. 'Fighting for Identity: the Funerary Commemoration of Italian Gladiators'. *Bulletin of the Institute of Classical Studies* 73. 2000, 93-114.

Hope, V. M. and Marshall, E. (eds) *Death and Disease in the Ancient City.* London and New York: Routledge 2000.

Hopkins, K. *Conquerors and Slaves: Sociological Studies in Roman History.* Cambridge: Cambridge University Press 1978.

Hopkins, K. *Death and Renewal.* Cambridge: Cambridge University Press 1983.

Hopkins, K. 'On the Probable Age Structure of the Roman Population', *Population Studies*, 20. 1966, 245-64.

Hopkins, K. *The Colosseum.* London: Profile Books 2005.

Humphrey, J. H. *Roman Circuses: Arenas for Chariot Racing.* Berkeley: University of California Press 1986.

Jackson, R. *Doctors and Diseases in the Roman Empire.* London: British Museum Publications 1988.

Jashemski, W. F. *The Gardens of Pompeii, Herculaneum and the Villas Destroyed by wVesuvius.* New Rochelle, New York: Caratzas Bros 1979.

Jensen, G. 'Private Toilets at Pompeii: Appearance and Operation' in S. Boss and R Jones. *Sequence and Space in Pompeii*, Oxford: Oxbow Books 1997, 121-134.

Kamm, A. *The Romans. An Introduction.* London and New York: Routledge 1995.

Kelly, C. *Ruling the Later Roman Empire.* Cambridge Mass. and London: Belknap Press of Harvard University Press 2004.

King, H. *Greek and Roman Medicine.* London: Bristol Classical Press 2001.

Kraus, T. *Pompeii and Herculaneum: the Living Cities of the Dead.* Trans. R. Wolf. New York: Harry Abrams 1975.

Kyle, D. *Spectacles of Death in Ancient Rome.* London and New York: Routledge 1998

Lachaux, J. C. *Théâtres et Amphithéâtres d'Afrique Proconsulaire.* Aix-en-Provence: Diffusion Édisud 1979.

Laurence, R. *The Roads of Roman Italy. Mobility and Cultural Change.* London and New York: Routledge 1999.

Laurence R. *Pompeii: The Living City.* London: Weidenfeld and Nicolson 2005.

Laurence, R. and Wallace-Hadrell, A. (eds) *Domestic Space in the Roman World: Pompeii and Beyond.* Portsmouth RI: JAR Supplementary Series No 22 1997.

Lefkowitz, M. R. and Fant, M. B. *Women's Life in Greece and Rome.* Baltimore: John Hopkins University Press 1992.

Levick, B.M. *Government and the Roman Empire: a Sourcebook.* London: Croom Helm 1985.

Levick, B. M. *Claudius.* London: Batsford 1990.

Ling, R. *Roman Painting.* Cambridge: Cambridge University Press 1991.

Lintott, A. W. 'What was the 'Imperium Romanum?'. *Greece and Rome* 28.1981, 53-67.

Lintott, A. W. *Imperium Romanum. Politics and Administration.* London and New York: Routledge 1993.

MacDonald, W. A. 'On the Expectation of Life in Ancient Rome', *Biometrika* 9. 1913, 366-380.

MacDougall, E, B. (ed.) *Ancient Roman Villa Gardens.* Dumbarton Oaks Colloquium on the History of Landscape Architecture X. Washington D.C.: Dumbarton Oaks Research Library and Collection 1987.

Matthews, R. *The Age of the Gladiators. Savagery and Spectacle in Ancient Rome.* Leicester: Acturus Publishing 2003.

McKay, A. G. *Houses, Villas and Palaces in the Roman World.* London: Thames and Hudson 1975.

Maiuri, A. *La Casa del Menandro e il Suo Tesoro di Argentaria.* Rome: Libreria dello Stato 1932.

Mau, A. *Pompeii: Its Life and Art.* New York: The Macmillan Company 1899.

Meiggs, R. *Roman Ostia.* 2nd edit. Oxford: Clarendon Press 1973.

Meijer, F. and Van Nijf, O. *Trade, Transport and Society in the Ancient World. A Sourcebook.* London and New York: Routledge 1992.

Millar, F. *The Emperor in the Roman World*. London: Duckworth 1977.

Millar, F. *The Crowd in Rome in the Late Republic*. Ann Arbor: University of Michigan Press 1998.

Miller, J. I. *The Spice Trade of the Roman Empire 29 BC-AD 641*. Oxford: Clarendon Press 1969.

Mitchell, S. *A History of the Late Roman Empire AD 284–641*. Oxford: Blackwell 2007.

Nash, E. *Pictorial Dictionary of Ancient Rome*. 2 vols. London: Thames and Hudson rev. ed. 1966.

Nielson, J. and Nielson, H. S. (eds) *Meals in a Social Context*. Ann Arbor: University of Michigan Press 1998.

Nippel, W. *Public Order in Ancient Rome*. Cambridge: Cambridge University Press 1995.

Ogilvie, R. M. *The Romans and their Gods in the Age of Augustus*. London: Hogarth Press, new edit. 1986.

Ormerod, H. A. *Piracy in the Ancient World. An Essay in Mediterranean History*. Liverpool: Liverpool University Press 1978.

Packer, J. E. *The Insulae of Imperial Ostia*. Rome: American Academy in Rome 1971.

Packer, J. E. *The Forum of Trajan at Rome: a Study of the Monuments*. Berkerley: University of California Press 1997.

Paoli, U. E. *Rome: Its People, Life and Customs*. Translated by R. D. Macnaghten London: Longman 1963.

Parkin, T. *Demography and Roman Society*. Baltimore: John Hopkins University Press 1992.

Peachin, M. *Frontinus and the Curae of the Curator Aquarum*. Stuttgart: Steiner 2004.

Pearce, J., Miller, M. and Struck, M. (eds) *Burial, Society and Context in the Roman World*. Oxford: Oxbow Books 2000.

Percival, J. *The Roman Villa: An Historical introduction*. London: Batsford 1975.

Potter, D. S. *A Companion to the Roman Empire*. Oxford: Blackwell 2006.

Potter, D. *Emperors of Rome*. London: Quercus 2007

Potter, D. S. and Mattingly, D. J. *Life, Death and Entertainment in the Roman Empire*. Ann Arbor: University of Michigan Press 1999.

Rauh, N. *Merchants, Sailors and Pirates in the Roman World*. Stroud: Tempus Books 2003.

Rawson, B. (ed.) *The Family in Ancient Rome: New Perspectives*. London: Croom Helm 1986.

Rawson, B. *Children and Childhood in Roman Italy*. Oxford: Oxford University Press 2003

Rawson, B. and Weaver P. (eds) *The Roman Family in Italy: Status, Sentiment and Space*. Oxford: Clarendon Press 1997.

Rich, J. and Wallace-Hadrell A. (eds) *City and Country in the Ancient World*. London and New York: Routledge 1991.

Richardson, J. *Roman Provincial Administration 227 BC-AD 117*. Basingstoke: Macmillan 1976.

Richardson, L. *A New Topographical Dictionary of Ancient Rome*. Baltimore: John Hopkins University Press 1992.

Rickman, G. *Roman Granaries and Store Buildings*. Cambridge: Cambridge University Press 1971.

Rickman, G. *The Corn Supply of Ancient Rome*. Oxford: Clarendon Press 1980.

Robinson, O. *Ancient Rome: City Planning and Administration*. London: Routledge 1992.

Rose, H. J. 'Nocturnal Funerals in Ancient Rome', *Classical Quarterly* 17. 1923, 191-194.

Sautel, J. *Le Théâtre de Vaison et les Théâtres de la Vallée du Rhône*. Avignon: Ruillère 1951

Saller, R. P. *Personal Patronage under the Early Empire*. Cambridge: Cambridge University Press 1981.

Saller, R. P. *The Roman Empire: Economy, Society and Culture*. London : Duckworth 1987.

Saller, R. P. 'Men's Age at Marriage and its Consequences in the Roman Family'. *Classical Philology*, 82. 1987, 21-34.

Salmon, E. T. *Roman Theater and Society*. edit. by W. J. Slater. Ann Arbor: University of Michigan Press 1998

Scarborough, J. *Roman Medicine*. London: Thames and Hudson 1969.

Scarre, C. *The Penguin Historical Atlas of Ancient Rome*. London: Penguin Books 1995.

Scobie, A. 'Slums, Sanitation and Mortality in the Roman World', *Klio*, 68. 1986, 399–433.

Scullard, H. H. *Festivals and Ceremonies of the Roman Republic*. London: Thames and Hudson 1981.

Sear, F. *Roman Theatres: An Architectural Study*. Oxford: Oxford University Press 2006.

Shelton, J-A. *As the Romans did: a Sourcebook in Roman Social History*. Oxford: Oxford University Press 1988.

Sherwin-White, A. N. *The Roman Citizenship*. 2nd edition. Oxford: Clarendon Press 1973.

Singer, C. E., Holmyard, E, G, Hall, A. R. and Williams, T. I. (eds) *A History of Technology, Vol. II*. Oxford: Clarendon Press 1956.

Speidel, M. P. 'Maxentius and his Equites Singulares in the Battle at the Milvian Bridge'. *Classical Antiquity* 5. 1986, 253–262.

Staccioli, R. A. *The Roads of the Romans*. Los Angeles: John Paul Getty Museum 2003.

Stambaugh, J. E. *The Ancient Roman City*. Baltimore: John Hopkins University Press 1988.

Stevens, S. 'Charon's Obol and other Coins in Ancient Funerary Practice', *Phoenix* 45.1991, 215–229.

Syme, R. *The Roman Revolution*. Oxford: Oxford University Press 1939

Talbert, R. J. A. *The Senate of Imperial Rome*. Princeton: Princeton University Press 1984.

Talbert, R. J. A. (ed.) *Atlas of Classical History*. London: Croom Helm 1985.

Tanzer, H. H. *The Villas of Pliny the Younger*. New York: Columbia University Press 1924.

Tilburg, C. van *Traffic and Congestion in the Roman Empire*. London and New York: Routledge 2007.

Todd, M. *The Walls of Rome*. London: P. Elek 1978.

Todd, M. (ed.) *Studies in the Romano-British Villa*. Leicester: University of Leicester 1978.

Toynbee, J. M. C. *Death and Burial in the Roman World*. London: Thames and Hudson 1971.

Toynbee, J. M. C. *Animals in Roman Life and Art*. London: Thames and Hudson 1973.

Turcan, R. *The Gods of Ancient Rome*. Translated by A. Nevill. Edinburgh: Edinburgh University Press 2000.

Vermaseren, M. J. *Mithras, the Secret God*. London: Chatto and Windus 1963.

Wacher, J. *The Roman Empire*. London: Dent 1987.

Waldron, T. 'Lead-Poisoning in the Ancient World'. *Medical History* 17. 1973, 292–299.

Wallace-Hadrell, A. 'The Social Structure of the Roman House', *Papers of the British School at Rome* 56. 1988, 43-98.

Wallace-Hadrell, A. *Houses and Society in Pompeii and Herculaneum*. Princeton: Princeton University Press 1994.

Walker, S. *Memorials to the Roman Dead*. London: British Museum 1985.

Wardman, A. *Religion and Statecraft amongst the Romans*. London: Granada 1982.

Warrior, V. M. *Roman Religion: A Source Book*. Newburyport MA: Forus Publishing/ R. Piullens Co. 2002.

Watson, V. M. *Roman Religion*. Cambridge: Cambridge University Press 2006.

Wells, C. M. *The Roman Empire*. 2nd edit. London: Fontana 1992.

Welch, K. E. *The Roman Amphitheatre: from its Origins to the Colosseum*. Cambridge: Cambridge University Press 2006.

White, K. D. *Farm Equipment of the Roman World*. Cambridge: Cambridge University Press 1975.

White, K. D. *Greek and Roman Technology*. Ithaca: Cornell University Press 1975.

Wiedemann, T. *Emperors and Gladiators*. London and New York: Routledge.1992.

Wiedemann, T. *Adults and Children in the Roman Empire*. New Haven: York University Press 1989.

Wilding, *Roman Amphitheatres in England and Wales*. Chester: Four Corners 2005.

Zanker, P. *Pompeii: Public and Private Life*. Trans. D. L. Schneider. Cambridge MA: Harvard University Press 1998.

INDEX

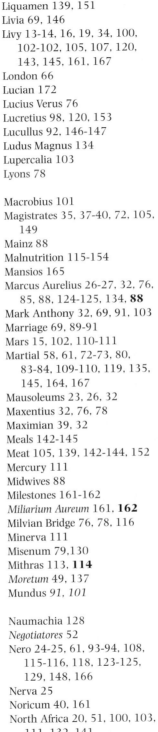